DOUGIE MACKENZIE

Mango Lassie

A MEMOIR OF THE SIXTIES

Jacket and title page illustration by Martha Sharer
Author photo by Kitty Leaken
Jacket and book design by Jeremiah Austin/DeNovo Creative
Printing by Better Impressions

Library of Congress Cataloging-in-Publication Data is available upon request.
Library of Congress Control Number: 2011938254

ISBN: 978-0-615-52266-1

Published in the United States of America by Loch Lomond Books, Washington, D.C.
www.lochlomondbooks.com

Publication date: 2011

To Mother and Dad

who sat through all the Elvis movies

"These Charming People"

*Donald and Millicent MacKenzie, with their children, Doug and Ross,
at Oatlands, Virginia (Washington Times-Herald, April 19, 1953)*

If the reader prefers, this book may be regarded as fiction. But there is always the chance that such a book of fiction may throw some light on what has been written as fact.

—Ernest Hemingway, A Moveable Feast

CONTENTS

Preface

Bruce Lee's big break came in 1964 at the Long Beach International Karate Tournament when Ed Parker asked him to give an exhibition of kung fu.

I had the good fortune to meet Ed Parker when I was fighting on the karate tournament circuit. This was the legendary Ed Parker who taught Elvis, and founded his first karate school in Utah in 1954.

It was September 6, 1980, and the tournament was The Lake Erie Karate Classic. It took place in Middleburg Heights, Ohio, a suburb of Cleveland. Ed Parker was conducting a seminar in *kenpo* the night before, so I thought I'd drop in.

The seminar was terrific. We watched Mr. Parker demonstrate rakes to the face and hand techniques that were part of his "alphabet of motion." When he asked if there were any questions, my hand shot up. "Our guest in the back," said the father of American *kenpo* karate.

"Mr. Parker, I'm not very big. So I'm not sure that hand techniques would work. I think *tae kwon do* kicks would be more effective."

I hadn't meant to sound confrontational, so I was surprised when the entire room turned and glared at me.

Ed Parker just shook his silver bangs, and smiled broadly.

"I haven't shown you my kicks yet," he said.

With this, he motioned for his assistant instructor to brace himself, and, KA POW! Ed Parker nailed the black belt squarely in the sternum with an explosive side kick. The poor fellow flew through the air and landed ass-over-teakettle. Wow! Talk about leverage!

Fortunately, the young man was very fit. He quickly righted

himself—no harm done. No one said a word. They had only to read the astonishment on my face to see that my conversion to *kenpo* was instantaneous.

After the seminar, I approached the sturdy young instructor.

"I'm really sorry. I didn't mean to get you killed."

He laughed disarmingly, flashing a smile that would've charmed the Theban stones.

"It's an honor to get kicked by Master Parker. It knocked the wind out of me. And I knew it was coming."

"That must've hurt," I said. "Tomorrow morning you're gonna feel like you were T-boned by a Buick."

"We get our kicks getting our kicks," he laughed.

By 1980, kicks had gotten harder to find.

You see, the greatest kick in my life had come five years earlier, in 1975, when I bought a car in Amsterdam with my girlfriend and drove it overland to India.

What an adventure. Try driving through the mountains of eastern Turkey on a dust-choked washboard road, with no guard rails, and room enough only for one car. Fearing we were going to die, I cried out as big trucks bullied our Fiat sedan. We recoiled when we saw the broken hulks of cars and buses that had gone over the road's edge, rusting like discarded toys on the floor of the canyon below.

After twelve hours of terror, we found ourselves in Erzurum where we were ambushed by two hooligans before we found our night's lodging in a filthy hotel.

In Afghanistan our first night was spent in Herat where we slept guarded by wild-looking Pashtoon tribesmen with antique .303 Lee-Enfields. They kept vigil all night below our porch on charpoy rope beds.

Our Fiat broke down constantly. It was so hot in Tabriz, the dashboard melted. We were caught in a landslide on the Jammu road to Kashmir. Dodging a boulder the size of a Volkswagen made my legs shake so violently that I couldn't keep them on the car pedals.

While writing a book of our Asia overland adventure entitled

Stopover Bombay, it hit me that I needed first to write *Mango Lassie*, about the passionate years that were the Sixties.

Who am I to write about those mad pursuits? Why me, you ask? Why not?

As that old cowboy Elmer Keith used to say:

"Hell, I Was There!"

Introduction

*I want a long straight road . . . and a car with the cut out
wide open speeding a mile a minute into the Sun
with a princess by my side..*
—Harry Crosby

I GREW UP IN COMFORTABLE CIRCUMSTANCES, a darling of privilege and
genteel luxury. I was driven to Middleburg, Virginia's Hill School by my
banker father in his beige Mercedes. It was a round-fendered "Ponton"
sedan with a hydraulic clutch and big Bosch foglights. The heater took
forever, so we froze on winter mornings.

Mom drove a '57 Ford, and its V-8 blew heat like a dragon's own
breath. It was a hip machine. Robert Mitchum drove one as a moonshiner in *Thunder Road*. That Ford was also my first car. I put Moon
spun-aluminum hubcaps on it and christened it "Road Rebel."

I could've been a moonshiner, too, only I had no sense of direction, asthma, and really bad allergies.

There was a small movie house in Middleburg, but we rarely saw
films there. My father's bald head was too tempting a target for gum-
drop-throwing miscreants seated up in the theatre's balcony. So going
to the cinema meant a trip into D.C.

There was scant traffic in 1957, and Dad drove like Juan Fangio
in that year's legendary German Grand Prix. Full chat meant a ninety-
mile-an-hour knuckle biter over Route 50's undulating hills. Northern
Virginia was a verdant vista of untouched farmland all the way to Fairfax.
Today, you'll encounter more red lights than a night in Amsterdam.

After our roller coaster ride in Dad's car, we were happy to be in D.C. Hell, after that hairy tear in the Benz, we were happy to be alive.

My brother Bruce was older and could read whatever he pleased. My little brother, Ross, and I made do with comic books, but never bought them. We were baseball crazed. Our money went into baseball cards. When we were small boys, Ross and I would trudge the three miles into town to buy baseball cards at the bus station. We loved the Middleburg of our youth when it was a sleepy Southern town of seven hundred. The main drag was lined with big shade trees, and we had two hardware stores. Now, the little hamlet is packed with trendy boutiques and tourists.

My father, Don MacKenzie, was an avid outdoorsman. He taught us to hunt, and fish, and ride our feisty Shetland ponies. Dad made sure we knew the name of every creature in the forest. When he took us canoeing, he'd whisper, "See that woodpecker. That's a pileated wood-pecker."

Dad was quite the naturalist compared to our down-home local folk. The country people couldn't distinguish a honey bee from a yellow jacket. Everything of that ilk was "a bee." And "a bee" was liable to get in your "cold slaw."

"Gall danged bee!" Mrs. Barker would shout as her trusty fly swatter smacked the dickens out of any insect that blundered into her bus station newsstand.

Everything to Mrs. Barker was "a bee." A wooly mammoth could frolic through town, but if it strayed into her newsstand, it was fair game. I liked Mrs. Barker. She combined the grace of an ox with the charm of a venomous reptile.

One day, when Ross and I were loitering at the newsstand, we discovered *Mad Magazine*. *Mad* was more risqué than any comic book. We huddled together and snuck a long, sniggering peek.

"Does your mother know you look at them books?" croaked Mrs. Barker in her jaybird twang.

We guiltily returned the magazine to its rack and hotfooted it out of there before Mrs. Barker mistook one of us for "a bee."

"Does your mother know you look at them books?" alerted me to the fact that certain books were taboo. I'd heard Brigitte Bardot described as "sexy," so I thought "sexy" meant cleavage. Cleavage gave me erections before I knew what they were. Girls my age produced the same effect.

One place I got to see lots of cleavage was on the covers of paperback books at Fluornoy's Rexall Pharmacy in Middleburg. Fluornoy's had an old-fashioned soda fountain where on a hot summer day we would enjoy a cherry smash or a chocolate marshmallow sundae. If my Uncle Burr was in town, we might even have a banana split.

The paperbacks at the drugstore were enticing. They cost fifty cents and sported lurid covers. It didn't matter what the book was about. It could be Perry, the Squirrel. The cover would feature busty squirrel tramps in a wanton pose, flanked by randy male squirrels. The background sketches would depict scenes of squirrel depravity. "Rodents From Hell," the cover would tout.

The cover of James Baldwin's novel, *Another Country* depicts a straight white couple gazing at the Manhattan skyline. The interracial couple in the book would've caused a furor in my hometown. Repression was the order of the day. Even the airwaves were segregated. My brother Bruce had "race records" by Little Richard. Little Richard wore make-up and screamed like a crazy woman. We white kids weren't allowed to buy his records, and Christian radio stations wouldn't play them. If we wanted to hear "Long Tall Sally," we had to buy the Pat Boone sanitized version.

Young men in my day didn't gun down their teachers and fellow students. We didn't play Doom or listen to music that degrades women and extols murder. We were God-fearing souls who believed in the traditional values of our Founding Fathers. We worked our fingers to the bone, keeping America great. And when we were weary, we rested. We were doers. We didn't sit around feeling sorry for ourselves. We were too busy getting wasted and nailing chicks.

We were the Baby Boomers—and we went boom boom all night long, brother. We didn't need Viagra. We had a ball, and made sure our women went home with a smile. They couldn't walk or talk, but they could smile.

Here's to you, gentle reader. May you smile, too, when you read this, and remember the Boomers, whose lives outshone the stars in that magic frisson of Flower Power... the Sixties.

Squeak from the Baby Corridor

When my cats aren't happy, I'm not happy. Not because I care about their mood but because I know they're just sitting there thinking up ways to get even.
—*Percy Bysshe Shelley*

I NEVER HAD MY RAP DOWN WITH CHICKS, so when I started getting lucky, it came as a surprise.

I went to military school when I was thirteen. While my friends were off to prep school, I flunked the eighth grade and wound up at Randolph-Macon Academy in Front Royal, Virginia.

When it came time to go away to school, I was assured that life away from home would be fun, like pony club, only I would spend the night. Oh, the new friends I'd make, and the jokes we'd share!

I still remember that first chaotic day at Randolph-Macon. Dad helped me carry my luggage up to my room. Then, he and Mom kissed me goodbye and drove off, praying they'd done the right thing for their darling boy.

What a shock it was that first morning when I shambled to breakfast with three hundred sleepy Sasquatches. Instead of chumming about with the chaps in *Chariots of Fire*, I found myself locked in Alcatraz with the cast of *Sling Blade*.

Still a child, I naturally brought toys with me. My favorite was an electric football game that vibrated and sent the players helter-skelter. The power was turned off at taps, so I consoled myself with blocking out plays in the dark. It was a lonely time.

I was the smallest boy—too small for an M1 Garand, so they issued me an old bolt-action Krag. The Krag—the U.S. Model 1898 Krag-Jorgensen—was the rifle that Atticus Finch used to dispatch the mad dog in *To Kill a Mockingbird*.

I was known as "the Mexican hairless" and hazed in the shower. I tried hiding out with the swim team so I could shower in my bathing suit. That dodge worked at first. But we had a mean senior who threatened us with a GI shower if we didn't shower on a daily basis.

Our tormentor went room to room just before taps. I could hear him coming down the hall, asking the first-year "rats" if they'd "had a shower." I would be reading my Bible with an angelic look when he peered through the door. This foiled him, or so I thought. One night he stopped and stared at me, sucking his teeth.

"MacKenzie," he drawled, "did you take a shower today?"

"Yes, sir."

"Who saw you?" he demanded flatly.

"Butch did," I replied, my heart thudding away.

I listened intently as he went across the hall to Butch's room to verify my story. When I heard Butch confirm he'd seen me in the showers, I breathed a sigh of relief. Butch Smith was a benevolent soul from Georgia, and I showered when he did. The instant I saw Butch in his bathrobe, I frantically peeled off my uniform.

The older cadets were a terror. The "rat" system empowered them to employ torture. One Saturday morning two of them dangled me by my ankles down a third-floor laundry chute while full bags of laundry whizzed past.

For us, there was no privacy, least of all in the head. The johns had no doors, and you let it all hang out in the showers.

The sight of so many naked boys all in a row was too much for our French teacher, Captain Irving Nightingale. "Nightie," or "Irv the

Perv," should've been singing "Where the Boys Are" with Connie Francis.

And he loved the showers. Wiping steam from his Coke-bottle glasses, Nightie would flounce down the line of cadets, squinting at tadgers. Then, he would call out a name and gape at each one as though he expected it to reply. The older boys used to mock him by holding theirs and making them talk, like Señor Wences. It was outrageously funny, and we laughed poor Nightie out the door in a panic.

Cadets fell out when they fainted. But I was the only idiot anyone could remember who had fainted at Federal Inspection in full dress uniform in front of Pentagon brass. I was carried to the infirmary, where I put down a story about having weak kidneys. No one bought it, least of all our school nurse, Mrs. Dove Zunk.

"Zunkie" was a world-weary pug with a puss like an angry cabbage. Her hair looked like someone took a can of spray paint and ruined a perfectly good hedgehog. Zunk was World War Two surplus, like much of the staff. Only Mrs. Kennedy, the librarian, was different. She was a Spanish-American War relic, like my bolt-action Krag rifle.

Our school physician, Dr. Blum, was a squirmy old codger with outsized hands and feet, like a character in an R. Crumb cartoon. Dr. Blum made his rounds every day after breakfast. I sat up in bed as he put a cold stethoscope on my chest.

"You're exhausted, young man. Aren't you sleeping?"

I broke down in tears. I couldn't stay awake through mess three. When I put my head on my plate, one of the redneck faculty wives conked me with a serving spoon.

"Stay in bed. Get some rest now, Douglas."

"Okay," I managed feebly.

"What's that you're reading?"

"*Another Country*," I said, "by James Baldwin."

Blum took wire-rimmed spectacles from his timeworn suit pocket. I think he had on the very same pinstripes the day Hitler bombed Antwerp.

"What's it about?" he asked pleasantly.

"It's the story of a Negro homosexual who kills himself."

Dr. Blum cringed. He put my book down like it was a dead snake.

"You're going to poison your mind," he warned sternly.

I was sipping my orange juice one morning when Nurse Zunk arrived. To my chagrin, the infirmary had drained of its real patients, exposing a tidal pool of screw-offs, notably me and Len Montalbano. Lenny was a jovial Italian kid with long eyelashes and a Roman nose.

"Tell Zunky you have the runs," advised Lenny.

"Why would I do that?"

"So she doesn't give you an enema."

Before I could reply, Lenny sprang out of bed and scurried to the safe haven of the bathroom.

"Breakfast in bed is not an occupation," declared Nurse Zunk sourly.

"No, it's an avocation," I said wearily.

I should've kept my mouth shut. The last thing I needed was a slanging match with a charwoman.

"MacKenzie," she drawled, huffing her bosom like a spinnaker, "when you get out of that shower, I'm gonna give you an enema."

"But I don't need an enema," I pleaded pathetically.

Arguing with medical staff is as futile as trying to beat up a cop.

"You get in that shower," ordered Zunk, who had the bedside manner of Zyklon B.

Lenny was suave. I was so twitchy, my school nickname was "Lizard."

"What are we gonna do, Lenny?"

Lenny didn't answer. He smiled inscrutably and went padding off in his flip-flops.

Lenny was the prince of the flip-flop long before Jimmy Buffett. The flip-flop is an important bit of kit. Essentially a rubberized member of the sandal family, the flip-flop endows its wearer with the cachet of a couch potato. Folks get out of the way when they hear the approach of flip-flops. That's because they respect the fact that the flip-flop wearer might be carrying an adult beverage.

I waited for Lenny for what seemed hours. Then, there he was, with a big smile on his face. He was carrying something, but I couldn't make out what it was. It turned out to be a brace of single-shot, disposable enemas.

"You won't believe what I told Zunk," he said, laughing. "I told her we were both shy about our bodies and that we'd be much more comfortable if we gave each other the enemas rather than have her do it."

"What did she say?"

He beamed triumphantly. "She bought it."

What a break! I breathed a sigh of relief as Lenny took each enema and squirted it into a big potted palm.

I didn't want to leave the infirmary. I was quite content to loll in bed, reading novels. But I couldn't sleep late, thanks to the idiot buglers who blew reveille at six-forty a.m.

I hated all the marching and endless drilling in the heat and humidity. I was also painfully homesick. I wanted to sleep in my own bed with my border collie, Shep. Shep was the sweetest dog. If he heard me crying, he would come up from under the bed and console me by licking my face.

Boarding schools make sure you never have a free moment. We stayed busy, cleaning our rifles or watching army training films about how to lance a boil or treat a comrade with a sucking chest wound.

Boarding school makes you fend for yourself. It gives you a leg up on your peers because you're thrown into the fray at an earlier age.

Boarding school instills discipline. You learn to take orders from dullards, and you learn to like it. You're the new boy, and you want to fit in. Only your new-boy status makes you stand out like Quasimodo in *Swan Lake*. Yet you fend off the jibes and the homesickness because you have to. You learn to adapt, and it makes you a better man.

Boarding school is where you learn to live like a leper and scrounge like a beggar. If you can survive boarding school, you can survive anything. Nuclear winter will be a snap. And you'll wear the appellation "human vulture" like it's the *Croix de Guerre*.

Life was tough. The second month of my first year—1962—saw

the Cuban Missile Crisis. Nuclear war seemed imminent. Then, in 1963, President Kennedy was shot dead in Dallas.

Jack Kennedy was our neighbor in Middleburg; his wife, Jackie Bouvier, had gone to Holton-Arms with my sister, Gail. The First Lady also foxhunted with Dad when he was a Master of The Middleburg Hunt.

One Sunday I sat behind President Kennedy in church. He was with his daughter, Caroline, and to me he looked like a movie star. I usually went to the Episcopal Church, but I went to mass that morning—at the community center—because my best chum, Ricky Patch, was the altar boy and I'd spent the night at his house.

It was exciting seeing President Kennedy, although, I must confess, I was a Nixon man—so much so, I had captained the Hill School debate team for Ike's beleaguered vice president.

Nixon lost the election, but we won the debate thanks to the quick wit of GOP classmate, David Barrows. Following the Democrats' impassioned recounting of Jack Kennedy's heroics in the South Pacific, David riposted with, "What does *swimming* have to do with being President of the United States?"

The audience roared and cast their votes for our Republican warhorse, who took the school election by a wide margin.

My third year at Randolph-Macon was hell. My brother Bruce committed suicide the day before my sixteenth birthday. Bruce was twenty-three. He'd graduated from Princeton, and he taught French for a year at St. Mark's in Dallas. Then, mostly to please Dad, he enrolled in law school at the University of Virginia. Bruce died in his dorm room from a mixture of alcohol and sleeping pills.

Ross and I refused to believe that Bruce could have taken his own life. Then, Dad read us the suicide note and described how Bruce's last cigarette had burned his fingers.

Up to this point, we had no indication that anything was wrong. My sister Gail confirmed that Bruce had shared some of his morbid ideations with her, but it never went any further than that. We buried Bruce in Rock Creek Cemetery. Ross and I wore our RMA uniforms.

It was the darkest day of our lives.

After the funeral, Ross and I were at home with one of Bruce's friends as we broke down Bruce's closet. "Bruce was a 'queer,'" the friend confided.

Ross and I were speechless. Being gay in 1964 ranked below being a communist or a cop killer. Gays in the movies dutifully bumped themselves off by the last reel. The only "good faggot was a dead faggot."

If Bruce had hung on a little longer, he would've felt the liberating Zeitgeist of the Sixties. Gay Pride was just around the corner.

CHAPTER

2

Angelheaded Hipsters

I've done everything but tango with a kangaroo.
—*Tennessee Williams*

PUNDITS POSIT THE SIXTIES BEGAN with the Beatles and ended with the fall of Saigon. A popular notion has Charles Manson, a self-proclaimed product of the Fifties, murdering the decade of Peace and Love. Another credits Altamont.

For me, the Age of Aquarius dawned one day in 1967 as I trudged up 'O' Street on my way back to my dorm from classes on the East Campus of Georgetown University.

My school chum, Peter Fletcher, hailed me excitedly from across the street.

"Hey, Dougie! Allen Ginsberg's speaking in Gaston Hall."

"When?"

"Right now."

We broke for the Gothic spires of Healy Hall. Peter was fast. He'd captained his prep school lacrosse team. I'd wrestled and anchored the mile relay. It was a dead heat as we sprinted past the statue of John Carroll.

"Let's sit up front," said Peter as we puffed up the stairs of Healy to stately Gaston Hall. "Some chicks are planning to tear Ginsberg apart after his poetry reading."

[13]

Terrific. Here was the guy who helped get William S. Burroughs and Jack Kerouac published, about to get ambushed by our self-righteous classmates.

The air in Gaston Hall was electric as we found room on the floor in front of the stage. We were bolstered by Father Richard McSorley and some Jesuit faculty behind us. Father McSorley wore sandals and spoke out against the war in Vietnam. When Air Force recruiters came to prey on us, he had their car towed.

It was unimaginable that we'd get to hear Allen Ginsberg.

Georgetown was so straitlaced in 1967. Georgetown men were required to wear a coat and tie to class. We weren't allowed cars and had to be in our rooms by eleven on weeknights and midnight on weekends. The Jebbies (Jesuits) were heroic beer drinkers, so they overlooked the beer and wine in our rooms.

Smoking pot in the dorm was out of the question, so we braved Kehoe Field at night and in the dead of winter. Icy winds whipped up from the Potomac River, making it hard to keep the pipe lit.

We never had any Beat poets at Randolph-Macon. Our coolest speaker was some guy from NASA. He had me don a space suit and hide in a fake space capsule on the gym stage. Awaiting my cue, I crawled out, to surprised laughter.

In his dark suit and tie, Allen Ginsberg looked more the courtly rabbi than a beatnik with a banned book. This was the same Allen Ginsberg who'd launched the San Francisco Poetry Renaissance at the Six Gallery.

That poetry reading in a converted garage on October 13, 1955, was an epic moment in American literature and the Woodstock of the Beat Movement. The featured poets were Phil Whalen, Gary Snyder, Allen Ginsberg, Michael McClure, Philip Lamantia, and Kenneth Rexroth, who would lend the reading gravitas by serving as master of ceremonies. Too shy to read, Jack Kerouac whooped it up, swigging red wine and beating his drum. The grand finale was a happily tanked Ginsberg reading "Howl" to a wildly appreciative crowd.

"Howl" put the San Francisco poets on the map. It also got

Lawrence Ferlinghetti busted when two plainclothes cops entered his City Lights Bookstore and purchased a copy of Howl and Other Poems for seventy-five cents.

Now, here was Allen Ginsberg reading us the same poem twelve years later:

I saw the best minds of my generation destroyed by madness,
       starving hysterical naked
dragging themselves through the negro streets at dawn
       looking for an angry fix
angelheaded hipsters burning for the ancient heavenly
       connection to the starry dynamo in the machinery
of night....

Allen Ginsberg mesmerized Gaston Hall. I've been to readings by Shelby Foote, James Dickey, and William Burroughs. None surpassed Ginsberg. When he finished reading, our Jesuit moderator invited the audience to ask questions.

"Yes?" said Mr. Ginsberg politely, acknowledging a girl in the back row.

"Are you happily married to a man?" she asked cuttingly.

You could've heard a pin drop in Gaston Hall. Her barb put everyone in the room on edge.

"I don't know what you mean by 'happily married,'" parried Ginsberg genially. "We don't fuck anymore."

We rolled on the floor, laughing at the would-be heckler.

I fell in with some friends as we bubbled out of Healy Hall on our way to The Tombs, a popular pub with Georgetown sports memorabilia adorning the walls. The Four Tops were belting out "Bernadette" from the jukebox while we scarfed down fat, juicy cheeseburgers and polished off frosty mugs of Bass Ale. I can't hear the song today without thinking, what a kick college was.

Before I saw Allen Ginsberg, I dreamed of driving race cars, like Scotland's Jim Clark. But after hearing "Howl," I thought being a writer might be the way to go.

Sitting so close to the stage to hear Ginsberg at Gaston Hall reminded me of my trip to Europe in 1965 with the American Institute for Foreign Study. I'd sat up front at a Parisian club called Le Sexy and wound up with a big wet mark on my white pants.

The French girls were lovely, and starkers, save for their G-strings. My friend, John, took the dancers in stride, but I didn't make it past the second girl.

I was sixteen and trying to lose my virginity in Place Pigalle. I'd had trouble finding a girl because I wasn't of legal age. In my camel hair sports jacket, white levis and weejuns, I looked twelve.

"*C'est combien?*" ("How much?"), I'd ask.

"*Trop jeune!*" ("Too young!"), they'd say, blowing me off.

I thought they were saying, "Trojan," so I produced a condom and waved it at them.

No deal. I eventually gave up and went into a nearby bar. That's when I spotted a hot little number dancing in front of the juke-box. She had on black clam-diggers and a frilly red top that bared her belly button. Nothing turns me on like a coin-slot belly button.

When Tom Jones finished "What's New, Pussycat?" I got up to play "Help!". Mademoiselle was leaning on the music machine, with her derriere angled seductively in my direction. I knew by her outfit she was not one of the Brontë sisters. My heart was pounding as I stood next to her and feigned interest in the music. She let her body touch mine ever so slightly.

"*Voulez-vous une cigarette américaine?*" ("Would you like an Ameri-can cigarette?"), I heard myself say in a schoolboy singsong.

A tantalizing jolt of pheromones hit me as she posed to adjust her hair. The sight of her underarms really zapped me. Hair under a girl's arms is sexy, but it's an art form lost on American chicks, who are brainwashed by Madison Avenue.

She took a cigarette and held it for me to light it.

"They're Camels," I said proudly.

She was puzzled. I showed her the dromedary logo.

"*Chameaux,*" I fumbled, employing a slang word for "scumbags." Her smile evaporated.

"*Je comprends pas*" ("I don't understand"), she said with a Gallic blow of annoyance.

My heart sank. Leave it to me to piss off a hooker.

"Camels," I pleaded. She stared with blank incomprehension.

I gave her the cigarette pack. She studied it gravely.

"Ah!" she piped exultantly. "Ca-MELS!"

Now she was all smiles. My hand shook as I lit her cigarette.

Coming on to prostitutes is no easy feat when you're sixteen. One time in New York I saw a skinny blonde I assumed to be a hooker. She kept pacing up and down in front of the Plaza Hotel.

"How'd you like to make ten bucks?" I asked.

"HOW'D YOU LIKE MY FOOT UP YOUR ASS?" she snarled.

Bonking a chick, especially a French one, would be a real feather in my cap, I thought, so I wasn't about to give up.

"*C'est combien?*" ("How much?"), I asked.

"*Quarante francs*" ("Forty francs"), she said.

"*D'accord*" ("Okay"), I agreed, throbbing with anticipation.

Pigalle's Hotel was a no-frills bawdy house with a pack of surly tarts manning the front door. I followed my new best friend into the lobby, where she picked up a clean towel and a key from the desk clerk. I could feel the blood hot in my ears as we went upstairs and took one of the rooms.

"Take off your clothes," said Mademoiselle, in French. I eagerly complied as she casually took off her slacks. "*Viens ici, chéri*" ("Come here, sweetie"), she ordered with a mischievous twinkle.

She lay back on the bed and took me in her arms. As we made love, she provided a play-by-play, which was lost on my high school French. Happily, I stayed erect throughout her narration; nothing can put you off your game faster than backseat driving. American girls are famous for this. The instant you're inside them, they start barking orders like Turkish fig merchants. What begins as lovemaking ends up as the rowing scene in *Ben Hur*.

French girls can say what they please. French is the language of love, and everything sounds great. Even the word for 'garbage can' (*la poubelle*) sounds melodious and sexy.

"*Oui! Oui! Oui! Oui! Oui! Oui! Oui! Oui!*" squealed Mademoiselle, reminding me of my guinea pigs.

"Ohhhhhh," I cried out, all too soon.

"*Ça va?*" ("Is it okay?"), she asked.

"*Oui*" ("Yes"), I answered.

When you're with a naked girl, it's like being at the circus. You never want it to end.

"Oh là là là là," clucked Mademoiselle as gravity compelled her to straddle the bidet.

Prior to Paris, I'd never seen a bidet. We mistook ours for a foot-bath and employed it as a beer cooler. My dimwad dictionary defined "bidet" as "a small horse."

This made about as much sense as the French. They put a bidet in your room but make you go to the john standing up.

"*Salut*," called Mademoiselle as she breezed out the door with a wry smile.

I bought a second-class ticket at the Pigalle Métro and scurried back to join my school chums at our hotel before anyone missed me.

I couldn't wait to tell my friend Jeff Ross that I'd bagged a smoking hot French chick. When I did confide in him, he emitted a terrible groan.

"I hope you used a rubber," he said solemnly.

"I didn't have to," I said beamingly.

Everyone was seated for dinner at the hotel and busily slurping up the soup course.

"You could come down with the 'black rose,'" warned Jeff.

"What's that?"

Jeff chewed the cheese from the end of his spoon. He assumed the air of a great tragedian.

"Once you've got the rose, your weenie is cooked."

I'd heard enough. I left the dining room and trotted upstairs. I filled the bidet with steaming water, and gave myself a painful wash. My minky didn't turn green, but it did turn bright red.

"You're never serious when you're seventeen," wrote the poet Arthur Rimbaud. I was sixteen and serious about finding a dream goddess, my mango lassie. My best picks were Edie Rader and Polly Hay, two chicks I'd met in France.

I first saw Edie Rader in the summer of '65 in Tours. She reminded me of Jeanne Moreau. We made eye contact while she was standing in line for dinner with some other AIFS girls. I gave her my best come-hither look, and she looked back! I was sixteen. She was seventeen.

Edie Rader was petite, and she wore her shoulder-length auburn hair in bangs. She had on a blue skirt and a white blouse. Her smart corduroy jacket and oxblood loafers denoted a prepster. Edie had a cookie cutter London Fog raincoat like every other American girl in Europe.

Chicks dress for other chicks, not us. If they dressed for men, you'd see nothing but cheerleaders and Playboy bunnies.

My wardrobe was Oliver Twist meets Gilligan and the Skipper. Edie's was more Goldwater Girl from the Borg cube. Granny dresses and rimless glasses were a long way down the road. So was my big fave, the halter top.

"Hi, there," I said, giving Edie my best X-ray eyes.

"Hello," she said, looking away.

"I'm Doug MacKenzie," I said, cutting the line so I could stand close to her. I was very forward, but Edie didn't mind. She gave me a look of appreciative wonderment.

"I'm Edie Rader," she said, shaking my hand. Her voice was soft and breathless, like Chet Baker on trumpet.

The dining hall was starting to fill up with hungry students. It was a hip cosmopolitan scene, with some African dudes in dashikis and others in sharp suits, looking very European. All of them spoke killer French. The bullshit racism that American blacks were hobbled with didn't affect the Africans. They came right up to you and started making friends.

"How do you like the food?" I asked, taking out a meal ticket. Our shoulders touched.

"It's so fantastic," she said excitedly.

"I saw you at Stonehenge," I said, "snapping pictures."

"I saw you at Buckingham Palace, throwing up."

"I was sick from the jet lag," I offered weakly.

"What jet lag?" she teased.

My second night of our AIFS tour, in London, had been a disaster. All the Randolph-Macon cadets gave senior, Richard Beck, money to buy booze. Richard, or "Old Bird Legs," as he was affectionately known, returned with enough liquor to sustain a Houseparties Weekend at Princeton. The next thing I know, I'm passed out buck naked and wrapped in a red velvet curtain in the hallway of our Bayswater hotel.

I was freezing, at five o'clock in the morning, and couldn't rouse my besotted comrades to open the door. I did manage to awaken everyone else in the hotel before the night porter came to my rescue.

"What's the idea locking me out of the room?" I demanded.

"Go to sleep, MacKenzie," said Richard groggily.

Everyone else was out cold. I put on some clothes and crawled into bed. At breakfast, I pressed Richard for an explanation. "How did I end up naked in the hall, wrapped in a curtain?"

"After the hard cider and the pink gin, you started screaming you were Errol Flynn. You climbed to the top of the curtain before we could stop you. Then you and the curtain came crashing down. You were lucky you didn't break your drunken neck."

The pink gin had reduced me to a raging hell beast, and our hotel room to a complete shambles. I'd fallen from an astonishing height and had been damaged only in the esteem of my fellows.

Richard sipped his coffee. He fixed me with an angry glare.

"Jesus, I'm sorry, man. I remember in the pub trying to buy John Player's Specials out of that fag contraption with the wooden drawers. It kept taking my money."

"You kept feeding it my money, MacKenzie. You lost *your* money."

Oh, dash! I'd started our school tour with five hundred dollars in travelers cheques and managed to lose them all within a day of setting foot on British soil. Fortunately, the lads at American Express were real sports about it. I didn't mention the pink gin, and they sprang for some replacement checks. What a bollocks I'd made of things— shades of Sebastian Flyte. I did penance by barfing at most of the major tourist sites.

Someone said that, to change the oil filter on a Porsche Carrera, you needed two elbows on your right arm. Let me tell you, if you'd dated the chicks I dated, you'd have needed two elbows on both arms. The preppy girls I grew up with were harder to score on than the '85 Bears. I'm not knocking them. They were really nice girls. They all let me kiss them and fondle their breasts. And that would be it. You'd spend all evening with the Easter bunny, only to go home without an Easter basket.

That summer I pitched more scoreless innings than Whitey Ford. Things got so bad, my hand had a headache.

I hoped things would be more promising with Edie. She was going to college in the fall, and that impressed me.

You see, I needed a girl who was both highly sexed and sexually experienced. That way, she could show me the ropes, and I could get my chops down. If Edie didn't pan out, there were lots of other American girls. Some of them looked like real sluts, too, so that was encouraging.

A fetching little item named Polly Hay had also caught my eye. We were at JFK airport, boarding a Saturn Airlines turbo-prop to Europe, and I made a beeline for her straightaway. Polly had a warm smile and architecture the Three Little Pigs could hide behind.

Sixties chicks were hot. They were a million times sexier than the current crop. Baby Boomer babes were all natural, too. Their bodies didn't look like they'd been mailed third class from Bangladesh—no tat- toos. I'm not keen on fake breasts, either. Breasts should be jiggly and hydraulic, not fixed and pneumatic. I much prefer a woman with small breasts to one whose boobs look like federally mandated bumpers.

I like a girl who's secure with her sexuality, and Polly seemed secure with hers—and everyone else's as well. She had a unique take on fashion, too. While the other AIFS chicks were decked out in their best vines, Polly wore a simple red dress that showcased her *belle poitrine*.

[21]

You don't have to be Charles Lindbergh to know that cleavage is an integral part of transatlantic flight.

I confess I wasn't mad about Polly's hair, which was piled as high as Beauvais—the highest cathedral in France. Nor am I a fan of finger-nails that look like they were purchased by Nosferatu at the all-night Revco. Maybe Polly confused Max Factor with Max Shreck. Once we were airborne, none of those things mattered.

In the dimly lit plane, Polly was romance itself. At thirty thousand feet she was peach blossoms in Verona after a spring rain. It was only after we'd landed at Gatwick that I realized that mascara is not a good idea if you're going to be up all night.

In the air, Polly was the sexiest thing on two feet. At customs she looked like a raccoon getting nailed on a morals charge. When she hailed me to help her with her gear, I feigned myopia and fled for the escalator. Once I hit the pavement, I beat it out of there like nobody's beeswax.

I know it wasn't chivalrous of me, ditching Polly, but it had to be done. In the brightly lit airport she stuck out like a hooker at high tea. The last thing I needed was for the other chicks to see me trying to nail Easy Cheese at the outset. It would've dimmed my chances with any of them for the rest of the trip.

Chicks dig it when you're aloof. If you come off as too eager, it puts out a pig-in-the-chow-line vibe.

The thing you have to remember about chicks is that they see how you fit into the scheme of things with other chicks. If you're in a relationship with one of them, they see you as a prize commodity. I know it doesn't make sense, but their biggest turn-on is taking you away from another chick.

If you're a dude, the last thing you want to do is bird-dog another dude's chick. When you bird-dog another dude's chick, you alienate all the other dudes—plus, you stand a good chance of getting your ass kicked.

CHAPTER 3

Blues for Mister Tadger

Ugh, ugh, ugh, my pigs 'tis in vain we tug,
I suck but no milk comes from the dug.
—*Percy Bysshe Shelley, "Swellfoot The Tyrant"*

TOURS IS A LOVELY FRENCH CITY in the chateaux country of the Loire Valley. The Loire Valley is an ideal place to learn French because it's reputed to be where the purest French is spoken. Parisian French is faster and full of slang. Learning French from Parisians would be akin to learning Spanish at a Puerto Rican baby shower.

Parisians are your pals if you're a lavish tipper. But they have a wide Tonya Harding streak and can turn on you like Dobermans in a hot car.

If you go to Brittany or Provence, the locals will give you the shirts off their backs. The French are *paysans*, and they have a big peasant heart.

The French are farmers. Idiomatic French is larded with the expressions of country folk who tend flocks and till the earth. How can you knock a country that makes three hundred kinds of cheese?

When Frenchmen die, they segue into the afterlife thinking about women. Jean-Paul Sartre confessed he "spent ninety-five percent of the day thinking about women." And he was a Nobel Prize laureate.

I really liked Edie Rader and couldn't wait to ask her out. When I called her up, she came to the phone all out of breath as though she'd just rushed in with a telegram.

"Hello," she said, expecting some big deal.

"Edie. Hey, it's Doug."

"Hi, Doug."

Edie was only a hundred yards away, in the girls' dorm, so we had a good connection.

"Would you like to go to La Chope after dinner?"

"Sure," puffed Edie.

"I'll pick you up outside your dorm."

"Are we walking?" she asked.

"It's not far. And it's a beautiful evening."

"We could go to the park. And watch the sunset."

"Groovy," I said casually, trying to contain my elation. "*Ciao.*"

"Bye, Doug," she said, hanging up.

In the summer of 1965, La Chope, a brasserie on Avenue Grammont, was the hangout for kids in my AIFS group. Bars in the States are bars. Bars in France are shrines. The French embody *joie de vivre*. No Frenchman on his deathbed ever said, "Gee, I wish I'd spent more time at the office."

La Chope has to be one of my favorite bars of all time. It served cold German beer on tap and ham sandwiches on bakery fresh *baguettes*. We American students would go to La Chope with store-bought bottles of Heinz ketchup and order *pommes frites*. Putting ketchup on fries really tripped our waiter out. I can still picture him bringing us steins of beer like a messenger from the Holy Land.

On our first date, Edie gave me a startled marmot look when I rounded the corner.

"*Bon soir, ma poule,*" I called out. "*Ça va?*"

Edie wore a blue summer sundress. She was flat as a Hemingway character, which suited me fine. Her gamine little breasts were very alluring.

"*Bon soir*, Doug," purred my date, with a smile.

"Wow! I like that dress. You look really tough."

In 1965, "tough" meant "sexy."

"*Vous êtes en pleine forme* (You are in fine form), Monsieur Doug."

"Thanks. I feel good, too."

I had on a striped sports shirt, white Levis, and brown loafers with white socks.

"*Est-ce que nous sommes à pied*?" ("Are we on foot?")

I gave Edie a lusty pirate kiss on the neck. She hugged me hungrily, so her breasts were against my chest.

"Cole and Linda Porter are taking us to the Ritz Bar for oysters and champagne cocktails. I insisted they not bring the Bentley. You know how it bruises your sable."

"*Ah! Mais vous plaisantez, monsieur.*" ("You're kidding.")

"Hey, cut it out, Edie. Speak English."

"We're here to learn French," she said as she clomped along beside me in her Girl Scout oxfords.

The instant we were alone, I grabbed Edie and really kissed her.

"Okay! Okay! We won't speak French."

I took Edie's bare arm and escorted her across the street. Strolling down Avenue Grammont, we were at ease in one another's society. When we passed a dress shop, she paused to ogle the latest fashions in the display window.

"I would never wear a pants suit," she declared resolutely.

"You have great legs. You don't need to."

"I have my dad's legs," she said proudly.

I imagined an amputee father pushing a little cart down the street with his knuckles. He might be one of those *mutilés de guerre* you were supposed to give your métro seat. You saw horribly disfigured people in France, especially in Paris. If you were a young American, you grew up without the grim reminders of two World Wars. For most of us, life meant the sunny side of the street.

Then, the Vietnam War came along, and we watched our generation get butchered on the nightly news. We ate our TV dinners while the sunny side of the street came home in body bags.

"I'm a Virgo," said Edie, out of the blue. "Is that good?"

I was being asked a question whose answer might determine whether I got lucky or not. Men are ill-equipped when it comes to traversing the no-man's-land of the female psyche.

"Excuse me?" I fumbled, feigning inattention.

"What sign are you?" pressed Edie. "I'm a VEER-go."

"Me?" I stammered. "I'm a Scorpio."

"I hate Scorpios," Edie said vehemently.

Oh, great. An astrological bigot.

"I'm not really a Scorpio. I'm on the cusp of Sadge."

Edie stiffened. Her eyes were angry slits.

"My last boyfriend was a Sadge. The two-timing slimeball."

"I have a Cancer moon. It negates the Sadge."

"What's your rising sign?" she asked suspiciously.

"Virgo," I replied apprehensively.

"VEER-go?" croaked Edie in astonishment. "I'm a VEER-go!"

It doesn't pay to have fixed opinions with chicks. Come off as dogmatic, and you'll end up tugging it solo.

"Do you believe in reincarnation?"

Now I was on the hot seat. Don't talk on the first date. Stay a blank screen for her fantasy projections. If you hold your tongue, your tongue will thank you later.

Do I believe in reincarnation?

I've delivered papers, picked grapes, washed dishes, bussed tables, cooked burgers, tended bar, moved furniture, spotted clothes, taught French, taught chess, cleaned toilets, and driven a laundry truck. I'm about as spiritual as Gordon Gekko running a pawn shop in Times Square on Black Friday.

But I'll gladly believe in leprechauns if it'll help me get laid.

"Funny you should ask," I said as we walked through the park into a cool evening panorama of flowers. "What about you, Edie? Do you believe in reincarnation?"

We paused to watch some swans gliding in a pond under a willow tree.

"I know I was a druid priestess," she avowed in an impassioned voice. "And I helped build the Pyramids."

"You must be good in geometry," I said, steering her towards a secluded spot.

We sat on a sun-warmed bench under a poplar tree. Edie spoke of wizards and dungeons and elves and warlocks and dragons and knights and gargoyles and stuff people buy at Renaissance festivals after they've smoked too much pot.

I sat entranced as she brought the fairies to life with such effect that I could see the pixie dust sparkling on their elfin slippers.

"IF YOU SEEK THE MAIDEN'S CAVE, FIRST YOU MUST SLAY THE DRAGON OF THE MISTY MOUNTAIN."

Hoo, boy. Night had fallen, and Edie was still yammering away like an Amway salesman on truth serum. By now, the elfin jive was bringing me down deluxe. Poor Mister Tadger had shrunk into his foreskin, and I had that numb feeling in my butt like you get in algebra class.

A guy always has a chance, but it's a puncher's chance. Chicks hold all the cards, so it's a snap for them to finesse us off the track. Ed Parker, the founding father of American *kenpo* karate, maintained that the difference between rape and rapture is salesmanship.

———

Most of my dates with Edie wound up in the park. We would start out sitting on a bench and wind up lying in the grass. One evening we were lost in some heavy petting when an elderly French lady reproached us for kissing in the park.

"Oh, Doug," moaned Edie as I fondled her breasts and slid my hand under her skirt. She was really breathing hard as I felt her soft inner thigh and white cotton undies.

"No," she said abruptly. "Not in front of the toads."

Sure enough, the park had filled with the adorable little amphibians. I thought of childhood summers and Shelley's:

The slow, soft toads
   out of the damp corners creep.

Edie was enchanted with toads. I was enchanted with her.

"Dougie, no."

"Let's make love."

"We did that already."

"What? We made love, and I don't remember?"

"We made passionate love in another dimension."

"That doesn't make any sense, Edie."

"Expand your horizons."

"Easy for you to say. You're not the one with blue balls."

"You're a big boy. You'll get used to it."

"I can't walk back like this, Edie. I'll ache with every step."

"Hop on one leg. I'll let you lean on my arm."

"I don't want to be seen in public with you."

"Why's that?"

"You're frigid."

Edie laughed. "I thought I was a cock tease."

"It's not funny. I'm in pain."

To my dismay, Edie put her bra back on and began buttoning up her skirt. Poor Mister Tadger was singing the blues so bad, he could've headlined at The Cellar Door.

Edie was all business as she stood up and tucked her shirttail back into her skirt.

"I need a girl who believes in free love," I resolved as our footfalls crunched on the moonlit pathway.

"You're an old soul, Doug. You've had plenty of sex in your animal lives."

If I couldn't make it with Edie, I needed to meet some new chicks.

And I knew just the place.

CHAPTER 4

Strangers When We Molt

A pretty girl naked is worth a million statues.
—*e. e. cummings*

LE KILT CLUB WAS A *boite de nuit* (nightclub) in Tours where teens met to dance and romance. We couldn't believe our luck when we found that French kids loved the same records that we did. I'd had a month of listening to bad pop music on Radio Luxembourg, so I was in the throes of a rock-and-roll jones.

Imagine my surprise when I stumbled into Le Kilt Club back in Tours in 1965 and heard Junior Walker blowing "Road Runner" on tenor sax. I made a beeline through the crowd and introduced myself to the deejay, a young French cat named Maurice.

Maurice Serres-Palson was a tall, wiry, pimp type with a blonde pompadour that made you think of a poor man's Phil Everly. Maurice must've been packing some serious meat because all the chicks got that glazed Martian look when Maurice strutted his stuff. Guys with huge puds don't even have to talk to chicks. They just splash on cologne, and the beaver comes in like Wild Kingdom.

Maurice was down with everybody. He had that sinewy El Greco look, like a lot of French guys. But he was no Alain Delon pretty boy by any stretch. Heck, Gerard Depardieu is better looking than he was. Maurice may have had narrow, slouchy shoulders and a bulbous

Adam's apple, but he also had that *je ne sais quoi*, and he needed to put that *je ne sais quoi* on a leash.

Maurice was a really happening deejay. He was no master of segues—he had only one turntable, and he had to bring in his own records. Paying for records took a major bite out of his income. Records in France weren't cheap, and a lot of them were imports. The French were big into EPs, and Maurice had EPs by the assload. EPs or "extended plays" were 45s with four songs instead of two. Putting two tracks on a single side of a 45 is a pain when you're cueing songs in a dimly lit deejay booth.

He played every crappy song on every record he had. Some of the Beatles' B-sides were memorably awful. The worst was called "You Know My Name." That's the whole song. The four moptops repeated, "You know you know you know my name," to fulfill a contractual obligation.

One Beatles B-side that turned out to be the hit of Le Kilt Club was "Mr. Moonlight."

I enjoyed making Maurice laugh. I'd wait for a romantic cheek-to-cheek and request "Coca-Cola Douche" and "River of Shit" by The Fugs. The Fugs was a Greenwich Village band led by Ed Sanders. Sanders, who ran the Peace Eye Bookstore, published the literary magazine *Fuck You.*

Ed Sanders went on to write a terrific book about Charles Manson. By then Ed Sanders was a solo act. The last recording by Ed Sanders that I remember was "Beer Cans on the Moon."

I was trying to become a solo act myself. I wanted to divest myself of Edie so I could date other chicks.

I really liked Edie. But her "fairy raps" were about as exciting as looking at pictures of naked girls after you've just jerked off.

There's no humane way of ditching a chick. Telling them you don't want to see them anymore is not the way to go. That only serves to make them want you more.

It's human nature to want what we can't have.

I started the ball rolling with Polly Hay on our student trip to the Basque country. I secured a window seat on the coach because I'd heard stories of French farm girls flashing our troops as they fought their way to Paris.

"Mornin', Doug," drawled Polly. "Mind if I join you?"

"Not at all. Make yourself at home."

This was rash. When Edie saw Polly, she was gonna freak.

"Stupid frogs," groused Polly. "They don't have closets."

"They have armoires."

"Hell. They don't even have laundromats."

"They have Brigitte Bardot."

Polly had on a straw sun hat and a purple Diane von Furstenburg cheetah-print wrap dress.

"The dumb asses never heard of Dr. Pepper."

"Oh, they've heard of Dr. Pepper. He's just not allowed to practice medicine."

Polly plopped down on the seat beside me with a groan. It was a hot day. The heat was taking its toll.

"If we were back home, I'd get me a Grapette."

"A six-ounce *Tiny*," I said. "They're the best Grapette."

I had helped Polly with her luggage, which was no small feat. She travelled with more materiel than Friedrich Von Paulus' Sixth Army.

"Do you have enough room?" she'd asked sweetly, wedging a cosmetics case between my feet.

"Sure. I had Toulouse-Lautrec legs, anyway."

Polly's boots were priceless. I thought of Dale Evans. Pretty Dale, and her horse, "Buttercup."

If Veronica Lake was *The Blue Dahlia*, Polly Hay was "The Purple Fuchsia," always shedding this, or losing that. I was a moron for losing my traveler's checks, but she trumped me by losing *all* her money, and her passport.

"I can't find my alligator bag."

"It's under the seat."

Polly smelled great as she sat beside me with her tanned knees deliciously apart. Her legs were wonderful, and never stopped moving. When she relaxed and rested her leg against mine, I became aroused.

So what does she do? She sits right in my lap.

"Are you comfy now, Dougie?"

"Me? Oh yeah."

Girls must know what they do when they sit in our laps. Polly knew. She was a Southern belle. Southern belles are schooled in Machiavelli by way of Margaret Mitchell.

"I hate wearing clothes. I love being naked. I want to splash in the Trevi Fountain, like Suzanne Pleshette."

"You mean Anita Ekberg?"

Polly pursed her lips in a wry pout. "What did Suzanne do?"

"In *Rome Adventure*?" I asked. "She went head over heels for Troy Donahue. He's a lovesick architect. When they spend the night, she makes him sleep on the porch."

Polly laughed a wheezy laugh. "That was so funny. When I saw that, I like to fell out."

"Emilio Pericoli sings 'Al Di La.' It was my brother Bruce's favorite song. I'm crazy about Italy."

"So am I," Polly said. "Italian's beautiful, and the men are gorgeous. They go after American women like Irish wolfhounds on St. Patrick's Day."

Polly fanned herself with a magazine. We hummed down a long road bordered with plane trees.

"Dumb-ass French," said Polly. "Their milk tastes weird, and their steaks are a joke. They don't even have Coke machines."

"I'm French on my mother's side, Polly."

"Go on. You are not."

"My mother was a deButts."

"A deButts? What kind of name is that?"

"You know, French Protestants."

"What's their claim to fame?"

"Well, for one, they saved a lot of Jewish children from the Nazis. Two of my ancestors were Mosby's Rangers. John deButts had a finger shot off. He took a bullet in the chest at Fairfax Courthouse.

"The deButtses are an old Virginia family. Descended from Henry of Navarre, the first Bourbon king. Here, have some bourbon."

"This is Woolite."

"It's Jack Daniel's in a Woolite bottle."

Polly took a yeomanly slug that made her eyes water.

Polly was a minx in the Fanny Brawne tradition. She griped about the view, the lack of lawn deer, garden gnomes and iron jockeys, before curling up in her seat, and dozing in my lap.

Traversing France was glorious in the Sixties, in those carefree days before superhighways. France was a bargain, and everyone carried Arthur Frommer's *Europe on $5 a Day*. We were drip-dry penny pinchers who washed our duds in the sink. French hotels never provided soap but often included a complimentary bedbug to suck any blood your taxi driver might have missed.

France was where you became an artist—where you frittered away your misspent youth. Then Mickey Mouse and Japanese tourists invaded Byron's "incontinent continent," and the snows of yesteryear were befouled by Ohio tourists wielding Lysol like latter-day Carry Nations.

I loved having Polly sleep in my lap. Everyone on the coach took notice, including Edie. Edie shot me a dirty look on her way to the lav. She had on a white tennis shirt and shorts so skimpy they hurt my eyes. I shot a sidelong glance at her slim little rump as it twitched down the aisle. It was a long ride, and I needed my late afternoon fix of java.

"Where are we?" asked Polly sleepily.

"Somewhere in France. You were asleep a long time."

"Sorry, Dougie. I didn't mean to drool on you."

"That's okay. You slept through 'Jimmy Crack Corn.'"

Polly moved my arms and sat up. She stared out at the gloom of a rainy motorway.

"What time is it?"

She took my left arm and blearily checked my watch.

"If we were in God's country, we could stop at Stuckey's."

"For a pecan roll. And some M-80s."

"No, stupid. For an orange Nehi."

"That's what's wrong with France. It has no billboards."

"They probably can't read," Polly scowled.

Polly intrigued me. Beneath the mannered sweetness lurked a sick mind. She would've been perfect for me, too, without the cosmetics. I knew she had a boyfriend back in South Carolina because she showed me his picture. "Do you think he's good-looking?" she asked.

I studied a photo of a chubby-cheeked boy with carport nostrils. He was wearing a football uniform and doing his best to look surly in a three-point stance.

"Biggy's had a crush on me since 4-H Club."

"Lucky you."

"Are you a 4-H'er?"

"No, I'm a 4-F'er."

"What's that?"

"Someone who doesn't want to die in a rice paddy."

Polly put her pictures away. She drew her knees up on her seat and sighed. I made a half-hearted attempt not to stare at her underpants.

"Virginia?" she snuffed. "I don't even consider that the South. When I think of Virginia, I think of the North."

"Richmond was the capital of the Confederacy. Virginia gave the South most of her generals."

"It's still not the South," Polly insisted. "If I can't see live oaks and Spanish moss from the verandah, you better lock me in the attic."

"Have you ever even been to Virginia?"

"I'm going to Sweet Briar College in the fall."

"You're going to Sweet Briar?"

"I was also accepted at Hollins. Don't act so shocked."

"Well, I never thought..."

"What? Do you think I'm an idiot? I happen to be an English major."

"Cool."

"There's more to me than the pep squad and the hop committee."

"You could be a little less Jackson Pollock with the old mascara."

Polly produced a compact and examined her face from every angle. I knew it was hopeless. It was the golden age of the beehive.

Women wigged up their hair like termite mounds.

"Would it disturb you, Douglas, if I painted my toenails?"

"No, not at all."

"A homecoming queen should always look her best."

"No argument here."

"Fetch me my cosmetics case."

I smiled, delighting in Polly's command of language. Only a Southern girl could use the imperative, dative and possessive cases in one sentence.

"I love how you look at me. Like the Big Bad Wolf."

I watched as Polly painted her toenails. It was better than a floor show.

"We could speak French. Like Russian aristocrats."

"That's okay." I said, holding up her left foot.

I stared longingly at the wispy tendrils escaping from their cottony confines. She had a thick shock of hair on her head. She would have one down there, too.

"France has changed me, Douglas. Changed me, forever. As God is my witness, I will never wear a beret again. And I look fabulous in a beret."

"It's not the end of the world. You can always wear a tam-o'-shanter."

She caught me staring at her undies and smiled playfully. I blew on her toenails and feigned indifference. Her eyes danced with triumph as she drew her knee back even more. God, she was killing me.

"I am going to be a poet," she declared. "Of course, I will suffer pitifully. Genius is a cross I shall have to bear."

"That rugged old cross. Maybe you could put those little suitcase wheels on it."

I couldn't see Polly as Sylvia Plath. I could see her as a frisky sorority girl. And I could visualize her with one breast bared, in a toga. But I could not see her clearing the high hurdles of metrical structure.

"There," she said. "All mama's little piggies are done."

"Who's your favorite poet?"

Polly batted her lashes. "Why, me, of course."

"Who's your favorite French poet?"

What an inane question. The French to Polly were a race of intractable mutants. She gave me a withering look and stared at the rainy vista with vacant eyes.

"I know. We could play Crazy Eights. Aw, shucks. I forgot my dang cards."

Polly stamped her foot in disgust. It was late in the day and the rain was really coming down.

"You know what I used to do when I was little? I used to take five of those green olives off the relish tray, and I used to suck out those little old red things, one by one."

"The *pimientos*?"

"May I show you?"

"Sure."

With this, she took each of my fingers in her mouth and slowly sucked them. I've never been keen on party tricks, but this piqued my interest.

"There. I've sucked *all* the little peppers."

"I can attest to that."

"So you know what I do next?"

My heart was really thumping.

"What?"

"I put an olive on each finger and wave to the adoring multitudes."

I pulled Polly down across the seat in the coach and kissed her hard.

Comrade With the Wolf

I never loved nor pretended to love her, but a man is a man,
and if a girl of eighteen comes prancing to you at all hours,
there is but one way.....
—Lord Byron

POLLY WAS A RESPONSIVE KISSER. We were in a dreamscape of love outside of Lourdes when we heard someone in the coach shout: "*REGARDEZ! UN ARC-EN-CIEL!*" ("LOOK! A RAINBOW!").

We broke off from our kiss to see a spectacular double rainbow.

I thought of Wordsworth's "My heart leaps up when I behold a rainbow in the sky."

Byron was never keen on Wordsworth, and he bridled when Shelley dosed him on the Lake Poet "even to nausea."

George Gordon, Lord Byron and Percy Bysshe Shelley are two of the most compelling figures in literature, and they were friends.

Shelley was striking. He was not only England's most lyrical poet since Shakespeare, he was also one of the most brilliant men that ever wore nankeen trousers.

Fluent in six languages, Shelley was noteworthy as a translator of Plato. Unappreciated in his brief lifetime, Shelley would never know the fame of Byron. Moreover, he would be cruelly disparaged, even mocked.

When his epic verse play *Prometheus Unbound* appeared, the joke of the day claimed he'd titled it "Unbound" because no publisher would print it.

Byron's pet name for his tall, shrill mate was "Snake," while Shelley called the endearing little clubfoot with his Scot's burr "Albè."

Byron's many mistresses and their resultant cat fights horrified Shelley. So did Byron's cavalcade of Venetian tarts. Shelley placed women on a pedestal. Byron found them more useful on all fours.

If Byron was a wolf content to be an outlaw, Shelley was an outlaw who wanted to reform the world. A high-minded revolutionary who launched pamphlets on balloons, Shelley preferred politics to poetry and reluctantly turned to verse because of ill health. Dismissed as an ineffectual angel, Shelley was no flake. He could be a rough customer when the need arose. No slouch with a pistol, Shelley went about armed. So did Byron, who carried small pistols in his waistcoat and consistently could hit oyster shells with them during target practice. Gentlefolk weren't so gentle in the brigand-fraught days of Regency England.

With no constabulary to keep the peace, travelers to London faced the fearsome prospect of a highwayman riding them down with a brace of large-bore horse pistols. These were highly perfected flintlocks that commanded respect. All you had to defend yourself against these lethal hand cannons were the puny coach pistols you kept in your carriage or on your person.

In this climate of easy crime, chaps could get downright trigger happy. Shelley was no exception. In Wales, he mistook his clothes on a chair for an assailant and put a bullet through them. Excitable by nature, and addled by laudanum, Shelley went so far as to convince himself that he'd contracted elephantiasis.

Yet, Shelley's voice comes through as infinitely practical in his letters to Byron. And he could be coolheaded when faced with an emergency. In one frightening instance when his wife Mary was bleeding profusely, Shelley had her sit on a block of ice, thus saving her life.

If there was blood lost in Lourdes, it was drained from the miracle hungry pilgrims by some of the more venal vendors.

Lourdes struck me as the gimp Las Vegas—Harry's Last Chance

Saloon for the terminally ill. I don't mean to imply that the entire town was a clip joint. Food and lodging were cheap. You could stay at the Grand Hotel Jeanne d'Arc for only twenty-seven francs a day *including* meals. Or have a four-course meal at the Buffet Du Gare for a buck, service included. What bugged me were the switchblades for sale with crucifixes on them. I may be wanting as a biblical scholar, but I can't recall Jesus switching a blade, not even on the moneylenders.

The Basques were nice as folks back home. Our waiters were fillin' station fast and fillin' station friendly. But Polly didn't take a shine to them, or to the miracle-seeking gimps all noodled over in their wheelchairs.

She was in a bad mood. When I bought her lunch, she griped about everything. I felt like Johnny Cash in his song where he's "buying store-bought cat food for a mean-eyed cat."

"If the frogs are so great, why don't they have doggie bags?"

"Come on, Polly."

Lourdes in the mid-Sixties was no romantic getaway.

I looked forward to Bayonne.

Bayonne was memorable because of Polly. She made Edie seem like a pony-tailed school girl. When I kissed Edie, I sensed I was merely an impediment to her next sentence. Edie was all talk and no action. Clearly, I had no use for someone that immature. After all, I was sixteen with a driver's license, and hair under my arms. Soon I would have whiskers and a car. The die was cast. The stage was set. I was ready to go all the way. My dry-humping, hickey days were about to end. Or so I thought.

I met up with Polly outside the hotel after dinner. She had on a low-cut titty top and smelled so nice she could've been made of pastry filling.

"Let's get blasted on the local vino," she proposed.

"What is the local vino?"

"If you're in Ravello, you drink Episcopio. It's the best red wine you've ever tasted. But they don't export it."

"Let's just get polluted. Out of our skulls."

"Rootin' tootin'."

We bought a couple of bottles of Fleurie. The man at the wine store said it was good. Wine in hand, we set out to find a nice secluded spot. I was content to stroll. Not Polly. She had some chick deal up her ass and took off like Wilma Rudolph.

"HEY! WHERE'S THE FIRE? I GOTTA CARRY THIS STUFF."

"Hurry, Doug. I want to see the crane."

I expected to see a wood stork. Instead, Polly was waltzing in twirls toward a yellow industrial crane. We'd slogged three miles to a construction site.

"Oh, perf," Polly laughed, plopping in the grass.

We passed the wine bottle back and forth. It was great, drunk straight out of the bottle. The night was mild. The air was fresh from the rain.

"Do you want to hear a poem?" Polly asked. She sat cross-legged, with her bare thighs and undies on display.

"Sure. What's the poem called?" I asked.

"'Satin Stan.' He was an old saddle horse we kids could ride. Stan was the sweetest horse."

I thought of the big white trail horse I rode once in Jackson Hole. He was so tame, he belonged in a petting zoo.

I listened quietly as Polly read her poem in the twilight of a foreign land. "Satin Stan" was free verse. I found it captivating.

"That's great, Polly."

"Honestly? You liked it," she said with surprise.

"I did."

Polly read her poems with feeling. One long one was about her father's death.

I quoted a poem I'd written after my brother, Bruce, died. It was called "The Bearded Man from the South." The last time I saw Bruce, he'd just driven home from Dallas in his white Corvair station wagon. He had given up his teaching post at St. Mark's School of Texas so he could go to the University of Virginia School of Law.

Bruce had little interest in law. He dreamed of becoming a writer in Milan, an Italian city he loved so much he had a map of it on his

COMRADE WITH THE WOLF

favorite jacket. Dad wouldn't hear of it. He had shelved his own dreams of Wharton to please *his* father. My sharpie grandfather railroaded Don MacKenzie into studying steam laundries. We were, after all, in the laundry business. Our family owned the Tolman Laundry in Washington, D.C. for a hundred years.

The last time I saw Bruce, I made fun of him. I'm afraid we kids all did. Bruce had grown a long beard that made him look like one of the Smith Brothers cough drop boys. I cracked up laughing the instant he stepped out of his car. I was only fifteen, but I've regretted mocking him ever since.

Polly read her poems until she ran out of light. Then she helped me polish off our remaining Fleurie. We watched the city lights of Bayonne come up before I kissed her. She was in an amorous mood and let me fondle her breasts. I might've done more than that, but I didn't try. It was a perfect evening, and I didn't want to spoil it.

I was taken with Polly in Lourdes and Bayonne, but when we returned to Tours, she started seeing my friend, Jeff. That threw me for a loop. So you can imagine what happened next. I wound up back in Edie's clutches.

Chicks do not take kindly to rivals. Edie griped that she was my consolation prize for losing Polly. I tried to mollify Edie with a *croque monsieur* at La Chope, but she had a real case of the ass. I bubbled with pleasantries, but nothing would penetrate Edie's snarl. Then, she really let me have it.

"I hear Jeff is squiring Polly all over town."

I tried eating my *pommes frites*. Edie would not stop.

"Jeff took Polly to see the nude beach movie."

"What are you talking about?"

"The Ile du Levant flick. Something *sans voiles*."

"Yuck."

"I heard it was *really steamy*."

"Well then, why don't you go see it?"

"Do you want to take me?" she asked. "I'll go."

Edie was being a real pain. She was smugly triumphant as we sat across from one another at La Chope.

"Those French girls let it all hang out. You might get to see Rudi Gernreich's Topless Swimsuit."

"Please leave me alone, Edith."

La Chope was filling up with AIFS kids. I wanted to be by myself in case Polly showed up.

"The girls say that Jeff is quite a stud," Edie needled. "He has the most alluring smile."

"I never noticed."

"He's so tall. And intelligent. He's gonna be captain of the football team. His mom's giving him a Toronado for graduation. What do you drive? Oh, that's right. A Corvair. Hee hee hee."

"Dad bought it for my brother and me. It's a Regal Red '65 Monza."

"Didn't your dad read Ralph Nader's *Unsafe at Any Speed*?"

"Fuck Ralph Nader. He's a joyless schlumpkin."

"Corvairs are death traps, Dougie. They roll over like wet dogs."

I pushed Edie's schoolbooks onto the floor.

"Why'd you do that?"

"They were in my way. Now stop bugging me."

Edie's eyes welled with tears. I tried touching her hands, but she snatched them away. The last thing I needed was a chick hissy fit. Lord Byron's Scottish mother flew into a rage after receiving an upholsterer's bill. This prompted her to have a stroke, and she dropped dead on the spot.

"You are making my life a living hell. Oh, Doug," she moaned. "What do you want from me?"

"I don't want anything from you. Can't we just be friends?"

"Friends? Oh, you are such a bastard."

I picked up Edie's books and tried to console her. You can't let chicks wallow in their moods, or they'll turn your life into the Sammy Maudlin Show.

Edie began to cry. Chicks are emotional surfers. And getting dumped is their North Shore. Their Pipeline. Their Waimea Bay. I needed to try a different tack. And fast.

"Edie," I said gravely. "I'm afraid I have some bad news."

She stopped crying. "What kind of bad news?"

"I joined a Satanic cult."

Edie's eyes didn't waver.

"You joined a Satanic cult? Is that all? Oh, God. You scared me. I thought you were gonna say you screwed Polly."

"I don't want you to be hurt, Edie."

"Hurt me if you must. I'm never leaving you. I'll follow you to the ends of the earth, Doug."

"You'll need an extension on your passport."

"I'll throw myself on your funeral pyre."

"I'm not a Hindu. I won't have a funeral pyre."

"I don't care what happens to us when we're dead, Doug. I just want to be a virgin for you on our wedding night, Doug."

"Stop repeating my name. Like a car salesman."

"Does that annoy you, Doug?"

"You annoy me, Edith. Now buzz off."

"Fine, Doug. I'm glad we could have this little chat. Now take me home. I'm feeling a little tipsy."

"I'm not going anywhere. I'm staying right here."

Edie stood, blinking at me.

"Would you like me better if I were a blonde?"

"I'd like you better if you were invisible."

Edie looked anguished. She was starting to lose control.

"Tonight is doo-wop night," I said.

"I'll wear my plaid skirt. With no bra."

"I'm gonna help Maurice get doo-wop records."

"And knee socks."

"Maurice is counting on me, Edie."

"I'll make your love beads melt."

"Stop."

"Then, it's a date? We can meet at the witching hour."

Edie's forced cheeriness started to wane.

She started to cry again. "I need a hug. Please."

Edie staggered towards me with her arms extended.

"You know you can never leave me, Doug."

I tried pushing her away, but she got me in a bear hug.

"Take me out with the garbage. I'm yours."

I fought to free myself, but she had dung beetle strength. "GET YOUR CRUMMY PAWS OFF OF ME, EDIE."

Now everyone in the café was staring. I tried prying her loose. She was all over me, like a jellyfish.

"NOOOOO!" she wailed.

Edie's face contorted, and was bright red.

"Please don't tear my new..." I heard the material rip before the words could leave my mouth. "...shirt."

Edie stood with the front of my shirt in her hands. Buttons clacked on the floor as I ran for the street.

It didn't end there. Edie dogged me that week like Popeye Doyle on "Frog One," in *The French Connection*. If I was at the *tabac*, Edie was at the *tabac*. If I chanced into the *patisserie* for a *réligieuse*, she would be there eating an *éclair* or a *chausson aux pommes*. If I went out for a *Herald Tribune*, Edie would be at the *kiosque*, eating a *gaufre chantilly*. *Putain*!

It was horrid. Running from her didn't work. She could catch me if I had a twenty-yard lead. Naturally, the more I tried to escape, the more doggedly she pursued me. Running from a chick is like running from a bear. You'll only trigger primitive instincts to chase you. And chicks have the patience needed for working jade.

I beat it back to Le Kilt Club.

"*Salut, grand chef*," I hailed Maurice, when I walked through the door.

Maurice was perfectly suited for doo-wop night. His tight pants and greased-back pompadour made him look retro '50s. He was a really good disc jockey and busted his nuggets to keep the dance floor hopping. I arrived at the club early while Maurice was getting his records together, and idly dicing limes behind the bar.

The club had a stale cigarette, sour cocktail smell from the night before. I helped myself to a beer and walked back to the deejay booth.

"*Oh, ze mozair fockairs*," grumbled Maurice. He had a *clop* in the corner of his mouth à la Jean-Paul Belmondo.

"*Bon soir*, Dogs." That's what Maurice always called me.

"How's it goin', bro?"

"*Au boulot*," he said resignedly. "I work 'ard my job."

"I work hard at my job," I corrected him.

"I work 'ard at my job, Dogs. But zey pay me no money."

Maurice shrugged. He puffed his cheeks and blew them out in disgust.

"Pff! Zese are my doo-wop *disques. Merde, alors*."

"Hey! Wow! Where did you get those cool shoes?"

"*J'ai des grolles en croco. I am now ze swingeur*."

I delved through Maurice's sucky records with dismay. The only doo-wop 45 he owned was "I Love You" by The Volumes. The rest ran the gamut, from Jacques Brel to Juliette Greco. I took a pensive sip of my beer while my friend took a long, soulful drink of his Pernod.

"Maurice Chevalier, Dogs. Ee ees for France ze beeg zinger."

"Who can't sing. He's a phony."

"You zink ee ees funny?"

"No. Phony. *Comme faux*."

Maurice tried to smile, but it was hopeless. Maurice Chevalier was not exactly on the DooTone label. When I think of doo-wop, I think of "In the Still of the Night" by the Five Satins. Or "Earth Angel" by the Penguins. When I think of Maurice Chevalier, I'm reminded of Woody Allen's line: "Those guys in the French Resistance were really brave— having to listen to Maurice Chevalier sing so much."

I had to do something. If Maurice lost his deejay gig, he'd get his marching orders back to *bidonville*—French for Palookaville. I had to act fast.

Cut to one of those Judy Garland/Mickey Rooney movies when Judy says to Mickey, "How can we bombard atoms, Andy? We don't have a cyclotron."

And Mickey blurts out, "My neighbor, Mr. Ferguson has a cyclotron in his barn. I'm sure he'd let us borrow it for our dance."

"Gee. Would he, Andy? Gosh. That would be swell!"

And so, good old American ingenuity would prevail. And the dance would be a smash. And they'd strike up the band because God always had an old machine when you needed it. It might be collecting cobwebs but, by golly, it would still work.

"I can get you some doo-wop records," I said.

"What are you telling me, Dogs?" Maurice asked excitedly.

"One of the chaperones has a record player, and a bunch of old records. I've heard him playing the Coasters and the Platters. I'll bet he'd lend them to me."

Maurice's head was a plasma ball of excitement.

"GET ZEM, DOGS! GET ZESE RECORDS FOR ME, RIGHT AWAY!"

I drained the last of my beer and stubbed out my cigarette. I was just about to haul ass back to the dorm when one of the potted plants in the window began to move.

It was Edie!

CHAPTER 6

Maurice Busts a Move

I'll make my heaven in a lady's lap.
—*Shakespeare, Richard III*

"**Maurice! Hide me!** I'm being chased by a psycho. *Elle est vachement dingue*." ("She is really nuts.")

Maurice was a Frenchman. I was under the impression that all Frenchmen had an arcane knowledge of women. Maurice picked the worst possible time to disabuse me of this notion.

"*Ce sont les femmes*." ("That's the way women are.") He blew hard. I stood, searching his watery eyes for help, but none was forthcoming.

I made a run for daylight, and ran smack into Edie. I tried to slip past her, but she put an Indian burn on my arm.

"*CA VA PAS NON!*" ("KNOCK IT OFF!"), I screamed in her face.

"Go ahead and yell. It shows you care."

I stared, in disbelief. Her eyes were black, as though she had suffered a *contrecoup* concussion.

"Jesus, Edie. What happened to you?"

I pulled her aside and examined her for bruises. She had on horrid red lipstick and ghastly purple eye shadow.

"I just came from the beauty parlor. What do you think? How do you like me now?"

"Does this beauty parlor have triage? Yipes."

Edie was wearing skimpy hot pants and a sheer top.

"I can see through that top."

"Well, feast your eyes," she retorted angrily.

"Why are you dressed like a *petite allumeuse* (cock tease)?"

Edie's hair was huge, but she was too wholesome to pull off the vampish look.

"You have on more makeup than Liz Taylor in *Cleopatra*."

Edie winced. "I thought you'd notice me if I dressed like Polly."

"Sorry?"

"If she dresses like a *pute*, I'll dress like one, too."

"I hate how Polly dresses."

A look of anguished surprise came into Edie's face.

"You do?"

"I *hate* makeup. Eyebrows are alluring. Yet women insist on mind-lessly tearing them out. You'll never hear a man say, 'Wouldn't Betty be prettier with more eyeliner?'"

"I thought you found Polly attractive because..."

"I liked you because you weren't dolled up like a mantrap, Edie."

"Then, why did you dump me? Polly has a steady boyfriend. She's practically married."

"Thanks, Edie."

"You're the laughingstock of my dorm, Doug. I had to tell you. I'm your friend. I can't let you go through life with your head in the sand."

Youch! Her words ripped me down the middle.

"I love how you take an interest in me, Edie."

"You do?

"Yeah. It fries my wig."

"I must be cruel to be kind," she said breezily.

I turned on my heels and left her sitting alone at the club. Then I hauled ass back to the dorm and made it to Hedgely Dalrymple's door, completely out of breath. Luckily, our worldly chaperone was there. I knocked hard in order to be heard over his record player.

Dalrymple was fond of blue blazers, topped with an ascot.

The first time I saw him, I thought he was a frog. He flounced into the dining area with a sweater tied around his neck and wearing his cowboy boots *outside* his jeans. This was the nelliest entrance since Peter Lawford waded ashore in *The Longest Day*.

Dalrymple's French was flawless. He correctly pronounced *"Hugues Aufray"* [oog ofray] and *"Les Halles"* [lay al] without an elision. Yanks invariably botch this. Not the Great Dalrymple, who made the most of his undergraduate education at Vermont's Middlebury College.

Finally, Dalrymple heard my knock over Frankie Lymon belting out, "Why Do Fools Fall in Love?" He flung open the door with a flourish. I was bowled over by the sight of Hedgely D. in one of those bathing suits no self-respecting male would be caught dead in. You know. Those thong deals that are no better than glorified jock straps. You might as well hit the pool with your po-po in a tea bag.

Before I recovered from this visual atrocity, I was hit by a cloud of cologne that made my eyes water.

"Hi, Mr. Dalrymple. How's it going?"

Clearly, I was the last person he expected. A mouse-like panic seized him.

"Yes?"

"Sorry to bother you, but I was wondering if I might borrow some of your records."

"My records?" he blurted with a guilty start.

"Your phonograph records."

Dalrymple turned down the music.

"What do you want with my phonograph records?"

"It's doo-wop night at Le Kilt Club. We could use some moldy oldies. Some Fifties tunes."

Dalrymple rolled his eyes. "I haven't many 'oldies,'" he said edgily. I stared at Mr. Dalrymple's feet. They were enormous. I felt like Wally Cleaver meeting Dr. Cyclops. "But help yourself to whatever you can find."

"Gee. That's really nice of you, sir."

I was thrilled with the 45s because Dally had lots of Dion. Dion was far and away the greatest of the teen idols. An Italian street kid from the Bronx, Dion rocked out with hits like "Runaround Sue" and "The Wanderer." In 1968, Dion would capture the spirit of the Sixties with his ballad, "Abraham, Martin and John."

When I finally made it back to the club, I found Maurice, already pie-eyed.

"I GOT THE RECORDS!" I hollered.

He couldn't hear me. The club in full swing was a mosh pit in a madhouse. I had to throw elbows like Patrick Ewing in the low post just to get across the dance floor. Maurice was in the deejay booth, doing the dirty dog, in god-awful orange slacks. He couldn't see me waving frantically from the moving sea of humanity.

"MAURICE!" I yelled.

Now he heard me.

"DOGS!" he hollered back. "*VIENS ICI!*" ("Come here.")

"*J'AI VOS DISQUES DOO-WOP!*" ("I HAVE YOUR DOO-WOP RECORDS.")

Maurice took the records and scrutinized them. When he saw what they were, he howled and gave me a hug.

"*TERRIBLE!*" he cried in French. He shook his hands wildly like they were wet, repeating "*Terrible.*"

Maurice was now bobbing idiotically, with his eyes squeezed shut and his teeth bucked out.

"DOUG!"

I heard someone calling my name. I recognized an American accent, but I couldn't pinpoint its source.

"DOUG! OVER HERE! DOUG!"

Jeff Ross and Polly Hay were sitting in a booth across the room, waving their arms at me. I gave Jeff the high sign and threaded my way through the crowd. I slid in next to Polly and savored the scent of her body as she kissed my cheek.

"What are you drinking?" shouted Jeff, pressing my arm down.

"French beer," I said, ogling Polly's mammary vista.

Jeff pinched his nose and made a face.

"French beer is so Michael Mouse. Have a Heineken's."

Beer was the last thing on my mind. All I cared about was Polly. And she was with Jeff.

"How can a country that's situated between England and Germany produce such wretched beer? It defies logic," Polly said.

She and Jeff were both embalmed, and they roared with drunken laughter. I laughed politely and looked up as someone forced their way towards our table. Edie! Before I could react, she hoisted a zombie glass and fired its contents at Polly.

"I HOPE THIS COOLS YOU OFF, YOU CRACKER BITCH!"

Polly weaved aside, and the drink caught me full in the face.

"ARE YOU OUT OF YOUR MIND?" I shouted, pulling Edie out of harm's way. Edie was seething with fury and trying to wrest herself from my grasp. Polly was a little powerhouse. She would have cleaned Edie's clock

Chicks! Take them out a few times, and they assume the guise of *generalissimo*.

"Thank you for ruining another one of my shirts, Edith."

Edie's eyes glistened. "I just wanted you to like me. I take it you don't want to make love to me?" She tugged on my arm. I wouldn't budge. "You want me, Dougie. You know you do."

"Hold that thought while I make a quick visit to the loo."

I started off in the direction of the lav, making sure that Edie was out of sight, and I circled back to the dance floor to find Polly.

There was my heart of hearts in the arms of my friend, Jeff. I watched as they glided by, bathed in colored lights. Polly hung from Jeff's neck while he kissed her, his hands on her rump. A numbing sense of inadequacy overwhelmed me. Seeing Polly dancing with Jeff triggered a host of dismal memories. So many times I'd watched the tall people dance while I looked on from the sidelines.

Maurice was not someone who could leave a tender moment alone, not for a minute. With a slow number playing, he was no longer the center of attention. He responded by making wheezing walrus noises in an open mike. Or he interpolated bawdy lyrics in the middle of

Francois Deguelt's *"Le Ciel, Le Soleil, et La Mer"* ("The Sky, the Sun, and the Sea").

I was immersed in a gargantuan sadness when Edie found me again. "Doug, do you want to go to the park?"

I'd had my fill of Polly and Jeff. I followed Edie's darling derriere through the club and out the door.

"Any more crazy stuff, and you're history," I said.

"Yes, SIR!" she barked with a neat Kay Summersby salute.

George Bernard Shaw said that only a young man can perceive any difference in young women. This is probably true. But you'll never convince a young man of it. For my part, I was so hopelessly mired in my adoration of Polly that Edie scarcely registered a blip on my radar screen. Had I possessed an older man's wisdom, I would've put Polly out of my head and adopted a more practical Stephen Stills "Love the One You're With" attitude—which, as it turned out, was pretty much what happened, anyway.

When Mademoiselle Rader and I arrived at the park, we were dismayed to discover every gate padlocked for the night. Undeterred, Edie deftly grabbed the top of the fence and nimbly vaulted over. I came clambering clumsily behind her and felt my feet sink into the soft cushion of a flower bed.

"YAAAAA!" whooped Edie. "THERE'S NO ONE HERE!"

"Sssssh!" I exhorted her. "You'll wake the dead."

"What dead?"

"Honoré de Balzac, for one."

"Screw Honoré de Balzac."

"Keep it up, and you might get the chance."

Edie was rambunctious. She shrieked, squealed and bounced around on her toes. I couldn't tell if she was drunk or just showing off.

"Edie. I'm kind of in a bind. I let Maurice borrow some of Mr. Dalrymple's 45s. We've got to..."

"Let's lie on the grass, Dougie."

Abruptly she pressed her wet mouth on mine, and I could taste the wine on her breath as she kissed me the way a red-blooded American boy loves to be kissed.

"But, Mr. Dalrymple..."

"That little *finocchio*?" she laughed. "Who cares!"

The grass was dewy. So was Edie as we shared a long kiss that had me fighting back the inevitable.

"Oh yeah, Dougie. Just like that... mmmm."

We were deep into some serious petting when the almost unthinkable happened. I tried sliding my hand past her elastic Maginot Line—as I'd done so fruitlessly so many times before. Only this time Edie relented. She didn't stop me, and my hand slid home.

Edie didn't want me to stop, and I wasn't about to. I kept her on the edge of rapture for the longest time.

Girls love more foreplay than you would ever think possible. So, hang in there as long as you can. I gave it the old college try.

I was unbuttoning my pants and thought that Edie would respond eagerly.

Instead, her eyes widened with fear.

"What about Mr. Dalrymple's records?"

"Huh?"

"You're already in Dutch with the chaperones. Do you want them to send you home?"

She was putting her panties back on before I realized what was happening.

"Edie, what are you doing?"

"This happened to me once before, you know," Edie confided.

"I came *this* close to being screwed," she explained, holding up two fingers to demonstrate her point.

I was devastated.

I was numb. I was too stunned to reply. I returned poor Tadger to his lair and buttoned up my pants.

I'd given Edie a good half hour of rapture and all I had to show for it were some grass stains.

Edie took off, leaving me to hike alone all the way back to Le Kilt Club to pick up Mr. Dalrymple's records.

"I came *this* close to being screwed." A phrase that will live in infamy.

When I got to the club, it was wailing full stomp. I didn't see Maurice. This fruck me out deluxe. He still had Dalrymple's oldies. *Shit.* It was shaping into that kind of night.

I had to whiz something awful, but some yayhole had yorked in the jakes, making everyone wait. Then, with my bladder at critical mass, the lav door flew open, and some drunken loser practically fell on top of me. It was Maurice. He pitched face forward, like King Tut out of an ironing board closet.

"DOGS!" he gasped as I steadied him. "Oh, Dogs, 'elp me."

"What's wrong, man?"

"Dogs," he blubbered pitifully. "My wife... she eez left me."

Maurice's wife was a mega-loser, with wigged-out hair and a grating voice that would make a gargoyle cringe.

"Maurice, hold on. I've gotta piss like a race horse."

"You must 'elp me, Dogs," he pleaded, hanging from me.

I loved Maurice, but, God, he was a weepy drunk.

"Eet eez feeneesh my marriage for me, Dogs. *Terminé.*"

Maurice defied logic. He'd been hosing chicks like they were coming out of a Trojan horse. And now he freaks when his troll-doll wife jumps ugly on him? I tried talking to him, but he made no sense.

"I need those records back, man. Where are they?"

Maurice put his head on the bar and began sobbing.

"Your old lady will come back, man. Don't cry."

"She 'ates me, Dogs. She zinks I sleeps weeth zee ozair womans."

Maurice's sob story might have made a good country music record, but I didn't have time to hear it. I collected Mr. Dalrymple's 45s and made it back to the men's dorm with just minutes to spare. No one was about. Everyone was still out on the town or already asleep. I lay back on my bed and thought about Edie.

When I closed my eyes, I relived the sensations of foreplay the way you relive a day in the surf. Edie had let me put my hand in her pants, and that was pretty hot stuff.

I felt sad about Polly, but Edie's stock was on the rise.

Girls danced through my head until, finally, I felt exhausted. I stripped down to my undies and crawled under crisp, clean sheets with a feeling of victory. Then, I remembered the records. Drat. I switched on my gooseneck lamp and saw them on a chair. Thank God. I pulled on my pants and tiptoed down the dimly lit corridor to Dalrymple's room.

Hedgely Dalrymple answered the door, in his robe. He had a guilty look like he'd been playing Onan the Rotarian.

"Thanks for letting us borrow your records, sir."

I behaved the way teens do around adults. Mumbling, with averted eyes. A polite hand-off, and out the door like a bomb scare.

A hairy hand closed on my arm. "Not so fast, Douglas."

"Sir?"

Uh, oh. Any time spent with an adult was a drag. And any time spent with an openly gay one was a nightmare.

"I trust nothing got scratched."

"I took good care of them, sir," I lied.

My heart sank as Dalrymple closed the door, with me inside.

"Welcome to my palatial abode," he said with a courtly flourish. "Might I offer you a postprandial libation?"

I forced a smile as Dalrymple camped it up. His titter was high-pitched, a chickadee laugh.

"*UN BOISSON POUR LE DAUPHIN.*" ("A drink for the prince.")

"Gee. Thanks."

I sat nervously drinking Sancerre from a plastic Blanche Neige cup.

"You must love rock and roll," I stumbled.

"'Music frightful as a serpent's hiss.'"

"It has a good beat."

"Melody was murdered by it. Opera is the only music, dear boy. Italian opera."

"It is?"

"Have you heard Renata Tebaldi as Mimi? Toscanini discovered her, you know."

"Far out."

"So, Douglas. What's your favorite opera?"

"Oh, golly. Gee, it's really hard to say."

"I know what you mean. There are so many great ones."

Dalrymple planted himself on the edge of the bed and sized me up through heavy-lidded eyes. Poor Dalrymple. Here was a perfectly decent guy who'd never get his weasel waxed by a chick. What a sad deal. Life on earth is a salmon run at best. And he was a gay salmon.

"Have a seat," he ordered, plumping the mattress.

"I can't, man. I gotta crash."

If I'd had half a brain and better taste, I'd have fallen for Edie Rader instead of Polly Hay. But Polly was the distant cloud.

When Debutantes Ruled the Earth

The Sixties aren't over until the fat lady gets high.
—*Ken Kesey*

"**NOT AN UMBRELLA**. I'LL LOOK LIKE ELEANOR ROOSEVELT."

I knew I shouldn't have brought my parents with me on that crisp September day in 1967 when I enrolled as a freshman at Georgetown University.

"ELEANOR ROOSEVELT WAS A COURAGEOUS WOMAN," exploded Mom, an ardent Democrat. "AND KIND TO THE NEGROES."

"HER HUSBAND GAVE AWAY THE STORE," shouted Dad.

Dad was a sixty-one-year-old staunch Republican.

"FDR WAS A CROOK. AND SO IS JOHNSON."

"President Johnson is not a crook," retorted Mom.

"He called Bobby Baker his 'right-hand man.' And he's a crook."

Dad chugged off with my luggage. He could be operatic.

"DAD! WAIT UP!"

Don MacKenzie was hell and gone up the stairs of New North. I kissed Mom goodbye and took the umbrella. Mom was a petite brunette and a real beauty. She was Dad's third wife, and seventeen years younger.

I liked Georgetown. It had cool, big stone buildings and chicks in miniskirts.

"DON'T FORGET YOUR HAT!" Mom said.

"JACK KENNEDY NEVER WORE A HAT."

"NEITHER DID HITLER."

I grudgingly went back to mom for the hat.

"Humphrey Bogart always wore his hat," insisted Mom.

Celebrity association was a favorite motivational tool. When Ross and I whined about having to wear shorts instead of pants, Dad screamed: "WHAT'S WRONG WITH SHORTS? THE MEN WHO DEFEATED ROMMEL WORE SHORTS. AND YOU SHOULD COMPLAIN?"

"Open an account at The University Shop," offered Dad.

The Georgetown University Shop was a swank clothing store. Sadly, it didn't survive the advent of the grunge heads.

"Okay, Pop. Thanks. Bye."

Fat chance. I dressed like Joe College that first day, and never again. I even accessorized my new suit with a briar pipe and a pouch of Cherry Blend tobacco. The pipe was my misguided approximation of a college man. Mercifully, I didn't show up in a raccoon coat with a ukulele.

By the time I made it to my dorm room, Dad was already chumming around with our hall Jebbie (Jesuit).

"Father O'Connor, this is my son, Douglas."

"Nice to meet you, Father."

Father O'Connor's laugh button was stuck. When anyone spoke, he'd cackle dementedly like a fun house clown.

"Douglas MacKenzie, a proud Irish name, to be sure."

Dad winced. He was proud of his Scottish ancestry.

Dad's grandfather hailed from Aberdeen, Scotland, so we were instilled with Highland pride. "If you're Scottish, that's half the battle," Dad liked to proclaim.

"Why, I'm Irish as Paddy's pig on me mother's side," I joked.

This tickled Father O'Connor. He laughed until his face turned red and white flakes fell from his head.

"Georgetown could pass for an Irish club," observed Dad.

"It could, indeed," cackled Father O'Connor. "But, lately, I've noticed a fair smattering of Italians."

I half expected Dad to scream, "Mussolini wore *his* hat!"

"I know you'll take good care of Douglas."

"That I will, Donald. I can see that he's a fine lad."

Father O'Connor wouldn't have known if he was on fire. He rarely ventured out of his room. Our discipline came from two law student prefects who lived at the other end of the hall. They were nice guys. One of them was named Maury. Mostly, they made us clean up puke.

Georgetown was an Irish Catholic club in 1967. Today, it looks like a Cairo bus station. The last time I was there I tried to do a sentimental tour of Copley Lawn where we'd played Frisbee, but the chums with footballs had given way to the junior execs with iPhones.

I walked to the new bookstore, threading my way through a sea of strange faces. So young and determined these budding women with their tattoos and laptops. Would they know what a Frisbee was for? Would they cherish Lotus Elans with their plywood trunks and oil leaks? Would they throw you their panties out of Darnall Hall?

—◦—

"Are you Doug MacKenzie?"

I'd half filled my dresser drawer with socks and undies when a young man appeared in the doorway.

"Hi! I'm your roommate, Don McNeil."

"Don, it's great to meet you." I said, pumping his hand.

Donald McNeil was a slight lad with an affable manner and an easy laugh. First semester he dressed like a junior Jebbie: black raincoat, chinos, socks, and oxfords. I liked Don from the jump. He hailed from Brooklyn and had the Flatbush sense of humor.

"I had my hands on her nipples," I told him, "and they were hard all night."

"Your hands were hard all night," Don quipped. "Maybe you should see a doctor."

Don McNeil and I were French majors—lucky that. Most of the

coeds were enrolled with us in the Institute of Languages and Linguistics, or "Ling Lang" as it was popularly known.

The toughest chicks in our Hit Parade were: (1) Katalin Almasy, a blue-eyed blonde with luscious lips and legs that stirred more than our youthful hearts. Katalin sat across from me in Dr. Pierre Maubrey's French class, ensuring I would be incapable of forming a sentence in any language.

"No wonder you're in love with Katalin," said Don McNeil. "Her belts are longer than her skirts."

"Come on. You don't think she's the toughest chick?"

"No way," Don said. "Susie is."

He fancied (2) Susie McConnell, a willowy brunette from Springfield, Virginia, now part of India.

Susie was a folksinger majoring in Chinese. When I put Susie behind the wheel of my Corvette, she took off like Danica Patrick in the Indy 500. When Susie McConnell boogied through the door of Dr. Richard "No Flunkin" Duncan's American history class, she had the male contingent of White-Gravenor ready for full-scale *amour*.

Another great pick (3) for Hoya teen angel of the 20th century was a petite, blue-eyed brunette from Rock Springs, Wyoming, named Kathleen Menghini. Kathy was so pretty I almost looked forward to French lab. Did I ever bonk any of these dream goddesses? Sadly, no. My love life was still languishing in its solid axle era. I was smitten with many damsels, but, alack, bedded none.

"Don, Jesus Christ. How can you just sit there reading away like some hellish zombie? What about chicks? I have a suggestion. We need a crash pad stocked with hippie chicks. If we were cool, we'd have teenage runaways bouncing off us like Flubber-crazed kangaroos."

Don gave me a withering look from behind his homework.

"And we'd have crabs bouncing off us, too, Charlie. Did you ever think of that?"

Don called me "Charlie." In his Flatbush accent, it sounded like "Cholly."

I was so horny I would not have made a good house pet.

In desperation to find girls, I joined two weirdo political groups, the YAF, and the SDS.

The Young Americans for Freedom were hardliner hard-ons who hated hippies and wanted to nuke Hanoi. They were the kind of secret-handshake buzz kills you'd meet at the pro shop. All I needed was an Alligator shirt and they would've bred me to their sisters.

And then there was the SDS. Students for a Democratic Society were mouth-breathing hairballs who wanted to blow up the science building. I had no interest in blowing up the science building, but I wanted a working knowledge of explosives so I could blow up the YAF.

Then, the coolest thing happened. Two letters arrived in my happy little Hoya mailbox. One was from Edie, and the other was from Polly. I scanned Edie's letter. It said she was gonna be in town that weekend. Boy, that got my heart started.

"Meet me Friday night at Union Station," she purred on the phone.

"Cool. I'll be there, Edie."

"I've changed since Paris, Doug."

I felt a creeping panic. "Changed? How?"

"Don't worry, silly. Only my body has changed."

"Shucks. That was my favorite part."

"Well, you haven't changed," she laughed.

Getting Edie in bed was a possibility if I played my cards right. Edie incarnated dogmatic. God forbid you had the effrontery to disagree. Edie was one of those people who went to college because they intended to become Emperor.

And her opinions resounded like edicts. When I cheerily touted a Camus novel we were reading in Dr. Johnson's English class, she dropped the portcullis. "No, stupid," she snapped. "Camus maintained that 'a novel is never anything but a philosophy put into images.'"

"Not necessarily."

"Albert Camus was a genius. You're a busboy taking freshman English."

"Thank you, Polyphemus."

"We are going to have fun together, Dougie."

"Bye bye, Edie."

"Goodbye, darling boy."

Now, Edie was coming to D.C., and, in a few days, Polly!

When Friday rolled around, I jumped in the Vette and drove to Union Station. Edie's train from New York was right on schedule. Edie stumbled through the gate in a miniskirt. I hailed her as she tilted toward me with her purse over her arm and an overnight bag in her hand.

Edie was attired in the go-go set look: white vinyl cap, matching grisette boots, and the dolly-bird fab gear that Jane Asher and Pattie Boyd Harrison had made famous.

"*Bonjour*, Doug!"

Edie's hair was cropped short, and she was in a neck brace.

"Wow! You look like... 'Twiggy.'"

"A boy on the train said I looked like Jean Seberg."

Edie laughed and gave me a big smile. When she put down her bag to kiss me, the momentum made her fall.

"SON OF A BITCH! WHO DESIGNED THIS PIECE OF JUNK?"

She kicked the bag in a rage.

"Are you crocked?"

"No. It's the stupid codeine. I took it with no food."

"What happened to your neck?'

"GIMME A SMOOCH, YOU HANDSOME POOCH."

"Ouch! Easy, man."

Edie laughed. She pulled me aside and Frenched my ear, which made me laugh because it tickled. I tried steering her in a straight line, but she tottered like a penguin.

"So how are things at Smith College?"

"Well, if you must know, they are a little too Sylvia Plath for me. LET'S GO TO CLYDE'S. I WANNA' BACON CHEESEBURGER!" Edie shouted.

"How did you hurt your neck?"

"I WAS DOIN' THE WATUSI."

"And?"

"I fell out of the go-go cage."

Sixties chicks were dangerous. They did crazy dances while doped out of their gourds.

"So, did you make the crew team, Doug?"

"Naaa."

Hoya Crew was a huge deal. When asked to try out, I was really elated. Then, I got the bad news.

"Wow, MacKenzie. You're tiny. You'll make a great coxswain."

Edie was blasting a doob before we'd made it to the car.

"Have a hit. I scored this from a spade cab driver."

"Put that shit out. Seriously. Cops are everywhere."

Edie made a terrible face.

"YOU BOUGHT A CORVETTE? I'M NOT RIDING IN THAT."

"How come?"

"YOU KNOW WHO DRIVES VETTES? REDNECKS AND FAGS," Edie screamed. "NO ONE IN THE HAMPTONS WOULD BE CAUGHT DEAD IN A VETTE."

"It's not just a Corvette. It's a 'Sting Ray.'"

"Gross. They even put 'Sting Ray' on the glove box. How tacky. Next time, buy a Jag, stupid. They're cooler."

"Thanks for the tip. I'll do that."

"Hey! That was Clyde's, man. YOU JUST WENT PAST IT!"

I couldn't take Edie to my place of employment. My boss, John Laytham, was Steve Straight Arrow. And his wife was a police officer. Edie looked like Giraffe Woman. And she was doing outtakes from *Reefer Madness*.

"Hey, Edie. Let's hit Little Tavern."

"Little Tavern? What's that?"

"It's a hip new scene where Joan Baez hangs out," I lied.

"ROCK AND ROLL!" screamed Edie like a mental case.

Little Tavern was out. It had stools and a floor Edie could fall on. Falling-down friends require special care which precludes hard surfaces.

"Let's go see the new 1968 Corvette. Then, we can eat."

"I'd rather go to some head shops," she griped.

"We will. The Chevy dealer is on M Street, right around the corner."

Be decisive with chicks, or they'll blow it for you. Fun for them can mean shopping for throw pillows at rush hour.

"I dig your outfit. I thought you'd be wearing a flowing cape and curled elf slippers."

"I look repulsive in this goddamn neck brace."

"You look fine."

We parked on 33rd Street and sauntered down the hill toward M Street. Parking in Georgetown was a breeze back then.

"Gosh, Edie. This is trippy, seeing you here. Two years ago we were kissing in the park in Tours."

"And you were trying to get in my pants."

"What do you mean 'trying'?"

Edie laughed disarmingly and squeezed my hand. "WHAT A KILLER DAY! GEORGETOWN IS BEAUTIFUL," she bellowed.

The instant we walked into the Chevy dealership on M Street, Edie let out a high-pitched squeal of surprise. "IT'S A FLYING SAUCER," she shrieked.

I could feel hostile eyes giving us the once-over.

"So, Dougie... what do you think?"

I wanted to love the 1968 Corvette, but its fit and finish smacked of slave labor. Plus, it was longer, heavier and uglier than the Sting Ray it replaced. It had no tech innovations, either. It had better aerodynamics, but nothing to write home about. Surprisingly, the new Corvette out-sold the vaunted Sting Ray. Buyers didn't mind the extra bulk—they loved it.

The Corvette has a special place in my heart. Burr MacKenzie, Dad's brother, drove a red '56. I'll never forget the other kids' faces when Uncle Burr drove me to Hill School in it. Man, what a sexy car!

"So, what do you think of the new car?" Edie asked.

I squeezed her hand when I saw a salesman headed towards us.

Car salesmen's antennae are tuned to the bandwidth of wealth. They do a quick hooker take on your footwear and grade you accordingly.

"May I help you?" he asked with ill-disguised contempt.

I had on Weejuns with white socks while Edie came off as "Bride of the Emergency Room" or "Easy Cheese Does Liverpool."

"Hey, I'm not your Kewpie doll," barked Edie as I gave her the bum's rush out the door back onto M Street. It was a luscious Indian summer evening in Georgetown.

"I hope 1968 turns out to be a better year than that car," I said.

Young Lady Chatterbox

*...Bosie and I have taken to hashish: it is quite exquisite;
three puffs of smoke and then peace and love. Bosie wakes up
at night and cries like a child for the best hashish.*
—*Oscar Wilde*

EDIE AND I WOUND UP AT CLYDE'S. We sat at a cozy window table and had bacon cheeseburgers and Bass Ale.

"Oh, this is charming," cooed Edie as we held hands across the red-and-white checked tablecloth.

Ian and Sylvia were singing "The Lovin' Sound" on the jukebox. Clyde's in 1967 was still an Irish bar.

"Did you notice all the motorcycles outside?" I asked.

Edie peered out the front window onto M Street at an astonishing array of British bikes: Nortons, Triumphs and BSAs, all the property of our studly staff. If a Honda 305 Super Hawk was in evidence, it belonged to a blaspheming freshman, you may rest assured.

"Dougie, who was your blonde friend who took our order?"

"Jimmy Ochs. He's a senior. From Dallas."

"He's really cute."

"I'll tell him you said so," I teased.

"Oh, no," flushed Edie. "Don't you dare."

We scarfed down our burgs with jackal abandon. Mine was

medium rare and just out of this world. I wiped the ketchup from Edie's mouth with my napkin. It was glorious being eighteen. We had nothing to do but drink beer. And we could drink some beer.

"That's one less sodbuster," I exclaimed, finishing another.

"Why do you call them 'sodbusters'?"

"It's from the movie *Shane*. Jack Palance guns down poor Stonewall, then, says, "That's one less sodbuster.'"

"You watch Westerns?" snuffed Edie.

"I love that scene in *The Magnificent Seven* when Steve McQueen says, "We deal in lead, friend.""

"I can't believe you're working as a busboy."

"We prefer to call ourselves 'busketeers.'"

Edie gave me a filthy look. Suddenly she looked awful in her neck brace.

"I'm not just a busboy. I'm a busboy at Clyde's."

Edie was cranky until the bacon cheeseburger and Bass Ale mellowed her out. I held one of her bare feet under the table and massaged her toes.

"That twisted my melon, man," she babbled. "Jeremy told Donna I was trying to sabotage their groove, but he's the toxic head case in this scenario, man."

"Don't hold down everyone else's groove, Edie. If you don't ignore Donna's chops, you'll always be her sideman."

"You didn't let me finish, man."

I had no clue what Edie was talking about. First, she plays the corporate automaton and grills my nads for being an underachiever. I mean, she covers everything from sewer bond issues to the price of pork futures. And now she's into some mindless rap about her brain-dead groupie sister, Donna, and Donna's Freddie Krueger boyfriend, Jeremy. Jeremy Ray was lead songbird for The English Sparrows, a local cover band. Edie's sister's name was Donna. So was Jeremy's sister, and his ex-girlfriend.

"Can you believe she said that? In front of Donna?"

"When she said what to Donna, Edie? I thought she was Donna."

Edie's eyes glistened with emotion.

"No, Doug. That was the other Donna, you moron."

"Wasn't she the Donna that got busted?"

"Donna didn't get busted. Donna got busted. Donna from Bethesda. Donna Donna, who got popped ripping Jeremy."

"Jeremy's sister, Donna?"

"His former old lady, numbwad. I told you."

"I thought Donna Donna was that Donna."

"What Donna?"

"That other one."

Talking to Edie was like trying to de-program a parrot. I listened to her Byzantine rants because I was a friend. Plus, I wanted to be around at the end of the date in case there was any sex.

"Did you invest in tax-free munis like I suggested?"

"Not yet, Edie. I'm waiting for my portfolio to thin out."

My eyes were at half-mast. The Clancy Brothers and Tommy Makem were belting out "Nancy Whiskey," my all-time favorite song on Clyde's jukebox.

I languidly smoked a cigarette as Edie lost herself in the lipstick ritual.

I was ready to drive home, to Middleburg. I wanted to get in the Plastic Pig and drive. True love is a hot rod Chevy on a starry night. With the top down you can hear the spring peepers and smell the earth.

It's fun stopping on a country road without another soul for miles. I remember taking Mandy Pringle to the drive-in in Warrenton, Virginia, and, then, stopping on the Zulla Road on my way home.

As I stood on the warm asphalt, I could smell the freshly mown hay as cattle lowed nearby from a moonlit meadow. The Band was singing "When You Awake" on my new Montgomery Ward eight-track cassette player. It was a stellar moment in the life of a young man. That entire evening was a minor miracle. Mandy was in the flower of womanhood. She sent me home humming.

Edie gave me a wild look and dug her nails into my arm.

"Oh, Doug! Did I tell you? My mother found my birth control pills!"

I could feel Tadger donning his RAF goggles and scrambling his Spitfire.

"You're on the pill?" I asked.

"A lot of good it does us in a neck brace," she said.

"You could take it off. How long have you had it on?"

"Dr. Mayfield said 'a week.' It's only been five days."

"Five days is a business week. And a doctor is a businessman."

"Gee, Doug," Edie wavered. "I don't know."

Edie sipped her coffee and eyed me slyly.

I tried to keep a poker face. My heart was on redline.

Love was wide open in 1967. You could be ravaged by green monkeys and suffer no worse than a broken heart.

"Okay," consented Edie cheerily. "Here goes nothing."

With that, she took off her neck brace.

"Hurray!"

"I was starting to feel like 'Whistler's Mother,'" Edie said.

Edie adjusted her vinyl mod cap. I snapped my fingers for Jimmy and the check.

Once outside of Clyde's we walked to the corner of M and Wisconsin.

"Where's the best place to get roaring drunk?"

We stared at the burnished gold dome of Riggs Bank. Truth to tell, I felt tipsy as we waited for the light to change. "I like a joint called The Bayou down on K Street. Their house band really wails."

"Are they called The English Setters?"

"No."

"The British Walkers? Are they the English Bull Terriers?"

"No. Why do you ask?"

Edie rolled her eyes. "Because most bands have something English in their names."

"No. The house band at The Bayou is The Telstars."

"Do they dress like Mods or Rockers?"

"Neither. They're local greasers with giant, teased pomps."

"But they're into the Mersey Beat?" puzzled Edie.

"No, Edie. The Telstars are red-blooded Americans. There's nothing English about them."

In 1967, the definition of "genius" was "anything English."

Putting the top down on the Vette was a snap. Edie helped with the latches and, presto, we were back on Wisconsin. We drove towards Foxhall along MacArthur Boulevard.

"Jeremy has hash," Edie announced confidently.

"Reefer?"

"No one calls it that anymore, stupid."

"Oh, sorry. I meant '*muggles*.'"

"Shitcan the shades. You look like a cop. Turn in here. My sister, Donna, is staying here."

We turned onto the paved driveway of an enormous house.

Volkswagen vans and ratty motorbikes were parked at odd angles: a sure sign the counterculture was in.

"I can't believe you wore those clothes. You look a fright. Don't talk. You're making me nervous."

"Why?"

"Maybe it's your hair. Or those half-fag shoes," said Edie.

"I could hide behind the door like Boo Radley."

Edie had to make a grand entrance for some glassy-eyed van dwellers and suburban burnouts.

"You're snapping at me," I said. "Like a Koochi dog."

"Quit crowding me, Douglas. Let me do the talking."

Edie was mighty assertive until she started knocking on the door. She pounded away on the door of the dignified old manse for a good ten minutes.

"Try the bell."

Edie tried the doorbell and sagged visibly when there was no response. She put her bag down and picked up a freshly delivered issue of *The Washington Star*. I took over at the door and pounded really hard. At long last we heard a yippy dog bark.

"That's Brynhild, Jeremy's dachshund."

"Edie!" cried Donna, opening the door.

"DAMN IT, DONNA. WE'VE BEEN POUNDING ON THE DOOR FOR..."

"Your outfit! Where on earth did you find it?"

"In the West Village," answered Edie gruffly.

"You must be Douglas. Edie's told me all about you."

Donna was hot. And high as a kite. She kissed me warmly, while Edie squinted like Teddy Roosevelt.

"How's life in Middleburg?"

"Great."

"Where's the poster boy for violent psychosis, where's Jeremy?" asked Edie.

Donna ignored her. She plopped down on a big comfy sofa beside a chocolate lab. The dog woofed and thumped a response with its tail as Donna stroked its mane. I caught my breath. Donna wasn't wearing anything under her shift. A tuft of flaxen hair peeked from between tanned thighs. Donna was giving me the glad eye as I fumbled to say something.

"Those are nifty shoes," I said.

"Thanks."

"Where did you find them?"

Donna let me lift each sandal so I could examine it.

"Madras," said Donna, accenting the second syllable. "They're made by hand from old tires."

Donna smiled at my unblinking stare.

"Watch the dickey bird," she said as she put her foot on my naughty bits and gave them a teasing jolt.

"What a charming house."

"It was," groused Edie, "before the Sparrows moved in. I cannot countenance a pigsty."

"Does this look a pigsty, Douglas?" asked Donna.

The living room looked like someone crash-landed a beer truck.

"No. Pigs don't drink Budweiser," I said.

Donna saw Edie heading over. She sat up while I made a hasty adjustment in my jeans.

"Douglas said I could spend the night at 'Journey's End,' his familial estate in Middleburg."

"My parents' farm," I corrected.

"I gather your parents let you cavort with your paramours?"

"So far."

"Groovy," said Donna.

She studied me with wide blue eyes.

"Maybe you could take me, too," said Donna.

"That sounds casual."

"Your parents wouldn't mind?"

"Of course not. We have plenty of beds."

"But your parents?"

"They *live* to entertain."

"You're sure?"

"Millicent and Don are the soul of good cheer. I practically grew up in a Noel Coward play."

"A Noel Coward play with horses."

Donna broke off as some footy hairheads trundled through the room without speaking.

"Not exactly the Von Trapps, are they?" said Edie the moment the hippies were out of earshot.

Donna started in her chair. "Why is Brynny barking like that?"

"I smell smoke," I blurted out.

"I smell it, too," said Donna.

"Holy mumpkins," cried Edie. "I think the house is on fire."

Straightjacket, No Chaser

When you go into yourself, go armed to the teeth.
—*Paul Valery*

Edie and I sprang to our feet in a panic. Donna seemed only mildly annoyed.

"Oh, wow, man," she said. "Not another fire."

Edie scampered off toward the kitchen.

"Do you have fires often?" I asked.

"Jeremy dries his jeans in the oven and spaces them out," said Donna. "Our neighbors get hyper and call the fire department."

"The next thing you know, they'll bug you about the axe murders."

Donna looked perplexed. "Jeremy's trying to book a gig for the Sparrows. But every time he gets on the phone, he nods out."

"Maybe he has iron-poor blood," I ventured.

Donna was unsteady on her feet. She walked with arms extended like outriggers as I helped her navigate her way through the furniture shoals.

Donna snorted. "I do everything, Douglas. All Jeremy has to do is get the band together, and he can't even do that. We've got a piano player who can't stride and a bass player who can't even play a G scale."

"And you're getting hassled by the fire department?"

"A few small fires, and they get all pissy."

"I know. 'The house is on fire,' pick, pick, pick."

"I'm baggin' some rays and they're like 'WHERE'S THE FIRE? WHERE'S THE FIRE?' I'm buck naked, right. What do I look like? A fire ranger? You should stay for dinner, man. We're gonna get pizza and watch *Star Trek*."

"What is *Star Trek*?"

A mystical serenity came over Donna. I had touched upon something sacred.

"It's the most amazing TV show. It's about these really cool space guys who roam the universe solving everybody's problems."

"It's like *Route 66*?"

Donna frowned.

"Like *Gunsmoke*?"

"No, dummy. They're on a space mission for peace. They stun you with their phaser guns, but they don't kill you."

"That sounds un-American."

"*Star Trek* is higher consciousness," said Donna. "And the chick crew members look like they're on a prime directive to get nailed. Oh, Wow. What was I doing? The house is on fire!"

The kitchen was a heavy scene. The acrid smell of scorched denim hung in the air. I observed the remains of mod bellbottoms in the sink. Losing your bells in the Sixties was akin to losing a limb. Your threads and your hair meant the world. I felt bad for Jeremy. He sobbed quietly in a rattan chair, with his shoulders shaking.

"Those were Jeremy's best bells," said Donna. "Everybody said they made him look like Jeff Beck."

"Shit, bro. Where am I gonna cop new threads?" whined Jeremy.

"I used to work at Woodies," I offered. "We had some pretty cool outfits in our 'Back To School' collection."

Malignant longhairs stared at me across the kitchen table. Their vibe was on the debit side of "hail fellows, well met."

Edie had made a mug of tea and was about to give it to Jeremy.

"Nothing hot," scolded Donna. "Are you ditzed?"

"Jeremy," said Edie, "did you meet Douglas?"

Jeremy was about as hammered as you can get and still be ambulatory. I made an effort to register on his radar, but no dice.

"Jeremy just woke up," laughed Donna.

Jeremy moved around the kitchen, in jerky starts, like a damaged android. His lips moved, but there was no sound.

"He'll be okay after he does some drugs," said Donna.

"What's he take?" Edie asked. "Re-animation syrup?"

"Let's hit the pool," said Donna. "I wanna swim."

"We need bread for the pizza!" said Edie.

A straw hat was passed around. The English Sparrows were all short of bread. I ponied up a sawbuck. Edie followed suit.

"I don't want a pizza," whined Jeremy. "I told you I wanted a macrobiotic dinner."

Jeremy's eyes were wide, like a hibernating animal that had been expelled from its den. Edie's demeanor was troubling to everyone. She opened pantry drawers and slammed them shut.

"Where's the aluminum foil?" she demanded, arms akimbo.

"In the pantry drawer," answered Donna.

Edie pulled a box of aluminum foil from the drawer and put an uneaten peanut butter and jelly sandwich next to it.

"Hey! That's my sandwich, man."

Edie saw her duty with clear eyes. She avoided Jeremy's gaze of blank consternation.

"HEY! THAT'S ALUMINUM FOIL, MAN!"

"Do you know what you've done?" whined Jeremy.

"Yes," said Edie. "I *wrapped* your sandwich."

"Aluminum foil is really bad for you, man."

Edie was ruffling the Sparrows' feathers. They glared at her with undisguised contempt.

"That was the last of the grape jelly, too, man," fumed Donna.

Edie had committed an unforgivable *faux pas*. She had desecrated a peanut butter and jelly sandwich. Peanut butter and jelly is sacred to hipsters, the way the pig is to the Polynesians.

"You fucked up everything, man."

The malevolence in the butler's pantry was palpable. In a South Seas movie, this was the scene where the white boys outran the outraged islanders, or wound up as long pigs at the luau.

"Well, I didn't know," wailed Edie. "I'm from Pennsylvania."

"You're gate crashin' my groove," said Jeremy angrily.

"We should go for a swim," suggested Donna.

Edie was on the brink of tears.

"I'll go upstairs and change," she said.

Donna took me by the hand and led me to the pool.

"I didn't bring a bathing suit," I said.

"Bathing suits bite."

With this, she pulled her shift over her head and stood before me, completely starkers. Donna had an all-over tan, and the sun made her golden hairs sparkle. She had peaky little breasts like her sister.

The sight of Donna's naked body imbued my heart with an ardor I wasn't getting in Father Francis Dinneen's linguistics class. We had a blast swimming in Jeremy's pool. If you've ever swum in the buff with beautiful girls, you know how life affirming it is.

I didn't mind if I had an erection with just girls around. But with guys present, I'd stay in the deep end while I tried to swim it off. I'd hoped Tadger might've shown more restraint in what should've been a nonsexual social function.

"Damn it," said Donna. "Have you seen my cigarettes?"

She padded around the heated pool, dripping water, while I employed my new towel rack.

"I should have a pack of Camels in my shirt," I said.

"Camels? They're even worse than Larks." With this, she bent over to look under an umbrella table and gave me her best vixen pose. Donna Rader was not someone you'd want at your sanity hearing, but, man, was she beautiful.

"Did you lose something?" asked an icy voice behind me.

It was Edie again. She had on a big sun hat and an old-fashioned, one-piece bathing suit that probably had been worn by Mamie

Eisenhower. I watched as Donna crawled around under the pool furniture.

"Donna lost her cigarettes," I shrugged.

"I saw you in the pool with my sister," said Edie angrily, "and you had a *hard-on*."

"How can you say that? I don't have a hard-on."

I pulled off my towel to show Edie. Tadger wasn't ramrod stiff. Then again, he wasn't taking a siesta, either.

"You have a mini hard-on now."

"I do not. How can you say that?"

"You were lusting for Donna and got an erection."

"What you saw was a mirage, an illusion of refracted light."

"I know what I saw, Douglas. Your minky was at high noon."

"It wasn't me. I swear. It was the *water*."

"Oh, sure. The water made you swell up like a sea monkey?"

A seismic thump came from the house as the air was rent with the shriek of an over-amplified electric guitar.

"Hot shit, mama," cried Donna. "The Sparrows are jammin'."

Edie looked bored in her *démodé* swimsuit. She jagged her hip to one side and rolled her eyes. The pool emptied, and everyone rushed inside like they'd announced the arrival of the Beatles.

"Do you want to go in and hear the band?" I asked.

Edie gave me a dark look.

"Don't worry. You'll hear every excruciating note from out here."

"She comes around here," sang Jeremy as the Sparrows went into a dyslexic rendition of Van Morrison's "Gloria"... "just about midnight."

Edie winced. I gritted my teeth. Worse was to come.

"G-R-O-L-I-A," wailed Jeremy like he was being tortured.

"*Grolia*? Is she from the East Bloc?"

"LET'S GO UPSTAIRS," Edie said.

"OKAY," I answered.

Edie's hash was the first hashish I smoked, and it was from Pakistan. It was hard and a shiny ebony on the outside.

"Smell it, Dougie."

I sniffed it appreciatively as we huddled on an upstairs bed. When Edie broke it open, it was green and soft.

"Isn't that the best thing you've ever smelled?"

The house vibrated with noise. The English Sparrows were making dreadful sawing sounds with their guitars, while squawking something unintelligible as a refrain. From upstairs, they sounded like angry parrots using lathes to grind the head off a cyborg.

"What kind of hash is this?"

"It's from Pakistan. It came through customs in a diplomatic pouch. This chunk came off a big *plaquette*."

"A what?"

"A big, thin brick stamped with the official gold seal of Pakistan."

"Is this the best stuff there is?"

Edie clucked dismissively.

"The primo hash comes from Mazar-i-Sharif. North of Kabul. It's the Holy Grail of the Hippie Trail."

"Wow. That sounds wild."

"Or the Blue Flower of early German Romanticism. You've read Novalis?"

"No. I can't say that I have."

"I think you're about to turn the page onto one of the most fabulous scenes of your life. Everything you've dreamed of is right over the horizon. Headed your way!"

"Cool."

"We'll smoke some. It'll be groovy," said Edie.

I locked the door and watched with doglike interest as Edie broke off little pieces to put in the pipe.

Edie slipped off her bathing suit and hung it on a towel rack in the bathroom. The bathroom was appointed in the art deco style of the 1930s. Glass beads glistened from curtains and on doorknobs. The bathtub was the size of the Queen Mary, and there was copious hot water the instant you turned the taps.

Edie assessed her image in the mirror.

"Look at me. Oh, God."

"What? You look absolutely perfect."

"My left boob is smaller than my right."

"You're ravishing. Right out of the box."

"I'm not exactly 'Playmate of the Month.'"

"No woman is, Edie. Those Playmates are all airbrushed."

"I look okay?"

"You look like a painting in the Louvre. Or the Prado."

"A painting by Goya." Edie gnawed her fingernails as she scanned herself in profile.

"Donna's the pretty one in the family. Everyone says so."

"Donna's all right."

"You'd like to fuck her, wouldn't you?"

I was so aroused I could feel the blood pulsing in every vein. I was on the edge of losing it, and Edie was bearing down on me for an answer. An answer fraught with peril. I tried to imagine what Fred Astaire would do. I could see him cinching his dressing gown as he bandied with Ginger Rogers. But Mister Tadger was too far gone for any zesty patter. I took Edie's hand and put it where I needed it. She did the rest. Her hand was adept, and felt great.

"Oh oh oh. I'm sorry. I couldn't hold it any longer."

"That's okay, Dougie."

"Your body is so beautiful."

I leaned against her smooth shoulder, feeling relieved and embarrassed. Edie gave me a soulful kiss and a reassuring hug. We stood for a moment, surveying the damage.

"Well," she said, "that's one less sodbuster."

Hot Buns in Search of a Coolant

Her lips suck forth my soul: see where it flies!
—*Christopher Marlowe*

"**You make me feel really sexy**," Edie said in a scratchy whisper, as we both sat, naked, on the bed.

"You are really sexy," I said.

Edie radiated confidence. She fondled her hash pipe with a smile I hadn't seen before.

"Pretty nifty, huh?"

"Sweet Jesus."

"No, silly. I mean the pipe."

I'd never seen a hash pipe. The only pot I'd tried was Mexican. An ounce went for fifteen bucks—but we never had a good enough connection to score more than a nickel bag.

"Oh, don't you love this song!"

What came through the floor was a seamless storm of amorphous noise. I had no clue what the dope-fried numbnods were playing. Trying to identify lyrics was like picking out musical phrases from a leaf blower.

"Is it the Blues Magoos?" I guessed.

"No," Edie scoffed.

"They're making a dog's breakfast out of whatever it is."

"It's called 'Just A Little' by the Beau Brummels."

"That was my next guess," I lied.

We were about to smoke hash and make love when a raucous VW bus pulled into the drive.

"Pizza!" shouted Edie.

Before I knew what was happening, Edie was wriggling back into her clothes.

"Don't you want to eat pizza?"

"You mean, now?"

I couldn't believe Edie would choose food before me, but she was so whimsical. Like the girls in grade school. You'd be talking to them one second, and in the next they'd whinny like ponies and gallop off together.

"We can eat pizza. And watch *Star Trek*."

We went in the kitchen where Donna was handing out slices of pizza on paper plates. All the English Sparrows were on the scene. Somebody had a Crystals record on. La La Brooks was singing "Da Doo Ron Ron" on Donna's new KLH Model 26 stereo. It was a groovy scene. The Sparrows were in fine feather. I was in a cool mood, too. Then, I saw my pizza.

"Hey. They forgot the cheese."

Everyone gave me the evil eye. Edie's glare was the worst. Her eyes were dead, like black sewing buttons.

"We didn't order any cheese, Douglas."

"How come?"

"We never have cheese, ever," Donna said.

"Why not?"

"Because they're mean to the cows at the dairy," said Jeremy.

"Oh, okay," I said, shrugging the whole thing off.

I bit into my pizza. It tasted like ketchup-flavored cardboard.

"*Star Trek* time," said Donna with a Moonie reverence.

I tried one more bite of pizza and dumped the rest in the trash. I imagined my Hoya cohorts at The Tombs, scarfing down juicy burgs in front of the jukebox. Johnny Rivers would be singing "Summer Rain."

"Jeremy's gettin' his shit together," Edie assured me.

Jeremy needed help tying his shoes. The few times I saw him awake, he had a perpetually baffled look, like reality was a pop quiz.

"The Sparrows might do *American Bandstand*."

Right. They'd be on *American Bandstand* right after Soupy Sales was on *Meet the Press*.

"Oh, righteous," cooed Jeremy. "*Star Trek*."

I fell in with a line of longhairs as we went into the living room to watch TV.

Great. I was abandoning the dreamscape of Edie's body to watch a TV show. To Edie, it was a big deal. She was so whipped up, you'd've thought Jascha Heifetz was coming to play a violin concerto just for us.

Jeremy and Donna sat on the couch with the dogs while Edie and I curled up at their feet.

"Are you comfy?" asked Edie sweetly.

"If I can hold you. Sure."

"Thank you for being kind to the cows at the dairy."

"Oh, my pleasure," I fibbed.

"Shelley was kind to animals. He would buy live crayfish at the market and release them in the river," I said.

"Ssssh. This is the cool part."

I cupped her breast and nuzzled her neck. Edie ignored me. She sat stock still, transfixed, as William Shatner intoned his hypnotic voiceover: "Space... the final frontier."

I thought I could endure an hour of little plastic spaceships. I'm a sci-fi buff. I was in the Science Fiction Book Club as a child, until they swamped me with unwanted books and my mom had to bail me out.

I sat through my first episode of *Star Trek*, which I wanted to watch about as much as I wanted to hear The Chipmunks perform *Parsifal*. Edie passed me the hash pipe. I took one hit and could not stop coughing.

"It's not cool to cough, man," needled Jeremy.

"Sorry, man," I said.

Jeremy giving tips on manners was like the Elephant Man sharing beauty secrets.

The hash was smoother than the grass, like a vintage Burgundy after retsina. Grass was good for a laugh and took musical appreciation to new heights. Friends were always turning up with the new Rolling Stones album. Or, turning you on to the best weed.

Star Trek seemed really bizarre. Kirk and Spock were dicking around on some planet while Spock tried to detect life-forms with some rinky-dink gizmo the prop guy probably made in shop.

"What are they doin' now, man?" asked Donna.

"Lookin' for that life-form dude," said Jeremy.

"What life-form dude?"

"The one that was hassling them on the *Enterprise*."

"Why are they doing that?"

"Because the show is called *Star Trek*, you stupid moron."

This ruffled Donna. "I know that."

"Well, they don't exactly stay home with Aunt Bee," said Jeremy.

Donna winced. I could feel Edie tense in my arms.

"We've seen this, man. This is the one where they get hassled by that bogus fishbowl-headed dude."

"No way, man. They're being hassled by the Greek life-form dude."

"What Greek life-form dude?"

"In the cocktail dress, man."

The Greek god life-form reappeared, as if on cue.

"Bitchin'," laughed Donna. "That is one humongous dude."

"He's a Greek god," said Edie authoritatively.

"WOULD YOU ALL JUST SHUT THE HELL UP?" cried Jeremy.

I was unstirred by the plight of the *Enterprise* crew, and, then, the hash took hold. Suddenly the prosaic drama took on profound inner meaning. The Greek giant wasn't a living entity. He was comprised of pure energy. And pure energy was a mind blower.

"Trip me out deluxe," said Jeremy. "The *Enterprise* is a magic bus. Captain Kirk is Ken Kesey."

"Who is Ensign Chekhov?" asked Donna.

"I think he's Mickey McGhee," I said. "Mickey was the Merry Prankster that Kesey called 'Stooges.'"

"This is heavy shit," said Jeremy. "Kirk and Spock are raising the consciousness levels of alien life-forms."

"That is so gnarly," agreed Donna. "I mean, WHOA."

Star Trek was groundbreaking stuff. It supplanted the Frankenstein of war with a new Prometheus of peace.

"They're in the future," said Jeremy. "America has evolved into a higher groove. Gunboat diplomacy went out with the twentieth century."

"They'll ruin outer space," said Edie. "You just watch. They'll screw up the entire universe."

Edie was cranky from the codeine. Yet, what she had to say was not far from the truth. Did Man belong in space? Humans have made a mess of the Earth. What if Man were to colonize Mars? In ten years, wouldn't it look like New Jersey? And what would happen if we encountered an alien civilization too advanced for lesbian Jell-O wrestling?

"Shut up, man," snapped Jeremy. "I don't talk during *Perry Mason*."

"No. You snore during *Perry Mason*."

Star Trek ended with a chorus of "Wow!"

"What's your favorite TV show, Dougie?" asked Donna.

"I like *Shindig*, *Hootenanny*, and *Hullabaloo*."

"Cool."

"I caught the Yardbirds on *Shindig Goes to London*. Keith Relf was wailin' on blues harp."

"Why did Eric Clapton split?" Donna asked.

"They got commercial. He was more into the blues.

"If Brian Wilson hadn't challenged himself artistically, we wouldn't have the *Pet Sounds* album. And without *Pet Sounds*, there'd be no *Sergeant Pepper's*. Paul McCartney said that "God Only Knows" was one of the greatest songs ever."

Edie stood up and stretched. "Dougie and I are gonna crash."

I left the room to trail Edie through the house and up the stairs.

"Are you zonked?" Edie asked.

"That was amazing. Thanks."

"Partying all the time gets old," Edie said.

"That's hard for me to believe. I wish I were Jeremy. He has everything: girls, dogs, hash, fun and freedom. I have a shitload of homework."

"Drugs are only artificial paradises. Anyway, they mess up your *jing*."

"My *jing*? What the heck is that?"

"Your natural essence. The stuff that keeps you happy every day. The real kick comes from the stuff we accomplish. When I'm at the end of my life, I want to look back on all I've achieved."

Edie laughed and dragged me into the bedroom. No sooner had we crossed the threshold than she kissed me deeply.

"It's hot in here. Oh, before I forget." Edie was half naked and searching for something in her suitcase. "Can't forget these," she said, taking out her birth control pills and taking one.

"Make love to me, Dougie," begged Edie. "I can't wait any longer."

11

Miss Rader Instructs

Show him no pity
He will come all the same
To drag you out by the heels
When the moon is full.
—*Laforgue*

A YOUNG MAID IN FLOWER is a sunburst of flesh. Edie was all that and more as we cavorted under the covers.

"Make love to me like I'm *Blanche Neige*, (Snow White)."

"I assume you don't mean the dessert?"

"Like a princess in a fairy tale," Edie cooed.

Edie was as impassioned as one of those wild women in Greek mythology.

"*Like that*," she panted, squaring like a wrestler.

The princess in my fairy tale wanted to *baiser en levrette*, or, literally, go at it like a greyhound. When a pretty girl goes on all fours, school's out.

"*Oui! Oui! Comme ça. Et plus fort.*" (Yes, yes, yes. Like that. And harder.)

Edie's body was a marvel. I looked at her and felt, the only thing that approached her rondure in finesse was a Jaguar E-Type.

"Gosh, that was awesome, Edie."

"How would you know? You're such a child."

"No way. I bag chicks like it's going out of style."

Edie laughed hard. "And you spend three minutes on each one."

"Did I do something wrong?"

"You could learn how to make a girl climax. I mean, it's not like splitting the atom."

"Oh."

"You don't even have your own place. You're a grown man, and you still live in the freshman dorm."

As a freshman I had to live in the dorm. Seniors like Bill Clinton got to share a house.

"I plan on finding more congenial lodgings, but I'm afraid my flurried social life keeps me a-go-go."

I pictured the crew back at my dorm, or "Fort Pecker Track": beer-muddled berks wallowing in a mire of emesis. The prospect of seeing them again did not gladden my heart.

"I love this room," I said, looking up. "I find high ceilings so reassuring."

"I do, too," agreed Edie. "I wish all bedrooms would hearken back to the age of the moguls. I could spend the entire morning, reading P. G. Wodehouse after a quiet breakfast of eggs Benedict."

"I'll bet this room has seen its share of sportive tricks."

"No one's spooned in here since Josephine Baker dazzled Paris."

Edie was so beautiful, she caught me off guard. Naked, she was the Rodin too daring for Rodin. Living goddesses have hair. Their marble counterparts don't do them justice.

Weren't statues originally painted? Now that makes sense. If Venus is going to be Venus, she'll need more than arms. She'll need that shock of geometric glory below her belly button. And she'll have to have that crazy little crack between her legs. Because that's the part that really slays you.

"What's your favorite memory of Paris?"

"I don't know, Dougie. Staying up all night and having onion soup at Les Halles. What's yours?"

"Seeing the Eiffel Tower for the first time. Watching the sun come up over Paris from Sacré-Coeur. A certain French girl who made me fly around like one of those ecstatics in a Marc Chagall."

"With you, it's always a 'certain girl.'"

Making it with a French girl was my fondest memory of Paris for a long time.

Then, one day, in the early 1970s, I had an epiphany while walking on the quay below Notre-Dame. I witnessed a miracle. It was the only miracle I'd ever seen, but it was spectacular.

It had been raining a lot, and the Seine was near flood stage. The great river was a muddy torrent that came all the way up to the quay. I was walking behind a woman and her small dog when disaster struck. The poor pooch strayed too near the river and fell in. The woman cried out in the most heartrending pain, but there was nothing anyone could do.

To everyone's amazement, two young Frenchmen sprinted downstream and readied themselves to make a grab for the drowning dog. One man had the other hold his ankles as he dove for the little dog and with impeccable timing snapped him out of the raging current, saving him from certain death.

I'll never forget the look of relief and gratitude on the woman's face when she had her beloved toutou returned to her, soaking wet, but alive. What a ballsy move that was! I couldn't believe what I'd just seen. As I walked around the Left Bank, I swear, my feet never touched the ground.

"I'm gonna be sore tomorrow," groused Edie.

"You are? About what?"

"I mean, my *body* is going to be sore in the morning."

"Yeah. But you're okay for now, right?"

"Oh, no. You're already hard again. That's really juvenile."

I was a monster of infamy, keen to have another go.

"Go ahead," said Edie. "I won't enjoy it." I watched as she angrily threw back the sheet.

I wanted to bonk Edie again, but her snarky tone put me off. A rat snake isn't venomous, but it can bite you in the eye.

"Gosh, Edie. I don't know what to say."

"You could say you love me."

Our calamus idyll was over. "Calamus" was Walt Whitman's pet word for phallus. Whitman was gay and openly so when Oscar Wilde visited the old poet at home in New Jersey, in 1882. Walt served his elegant guest homemade elderberry wine, which Wilde cheerfully imbibed.

Said Oscar: "If it had been vinegar I should have drunk it all the same, for I have an admiration for that man which I can hardly express."

"Oh, listen," Edie cooed. "It's raining."

"I left the top down. My car..."

"You're not leaving me?"

"I've got a linguistics paper."

"So?"

"I gotta get cracking so Father Dinneen doesn't play *jai alai* with my *huevos*."

"Water won't hurt your car. It's just crummy vinyl."

"I have a factory teakwood steering wheel."

"So?"

"Edie, I have to be back in the dorm, now. Or face Father O'Connor."

Our hall "Jebbie," Father O'Connor, was as ferocious as a field mouse and dead to the world by nine o'clock.

"You bastard. You can't just screw me and leave!"

I'd hoped to close on a clarion note, but, clearly, Edie was wrapped too tight for Free Love.

"Don't you dare leave, you little four-flusher!"

I thought the dope would've mellowed Edie. One of the big myths was that dope expands your consciousness. All we had to do was tab the warmongers with acid, and they would see the light and stop the bombing. A well-placed hash brownie and LBJ would turn into a hippie the way Peter Sellers did in the movie *I Love You, Alice B. Toklas.*

———◆———

It had stopped raining when I finally parked the Vette, back on Wisconsin Avenue. Britt's cafeteria opened at midnight for breakfast.

Britt's was an all-night hangout for hipsters and university night owls.

"Yo, MacKenzie!"

I heard my name over the hubbub as I loaded my tray with scrambled eggs, toast, bacon, orange juice, and coffee. Britt's was humming with Georgetown street life. I scanned the joint for a place to sit.

"Dougie," called out someone, in a patrician voice. "Over here."

Peter Fletcher sat alone at a table in the corner. He had on the same getup he'd worn to Dr. Dillingham's philosophy class: a black, Catholic-boy trench coat with a matching turtleneck. His black jeans sprouted motorcycle boots, giving the impression of an altar boy gone bad.

"All black? Are we Masha from *The Seagull*?"

"I smell coppers," hissed Peter. "Piggies *partout.*"

I enjoyed Peter Fletcher. He was one of the few kids on my hall who knew the score.

"I tried to cop some acid at the Silver Dollar," he said.

"Jeez, Peter. That's a shit kicker bar."

Peter naturally aroused suspicion. He ran a nervous hand through his blonde locks as he scanned the restaurant for narcs.

"Stumpy thinks he can get us some LSD."

"Who is Stumpy?" I asked.

"Shorty's best friend."

"Who's Shorty?"

"Shorty? He's a crossing guard."

"You're copping from a crossing guard?"

Peter was offended.

"They don't let just anyone be a crossing guard."

"I know. First, you complete commando school. Then, they boot you up to military intelligence."

"Very funny."

You had to take Peter's comments with a grain of salt. He was impressionable beyond belief. One week, he'd be set on becoming a missionary. The next, he'd be obsessed with UFOs. He was always flirting with cults, too. And poring over pamphlets a normal person would find ridiculous.

"Did you dine out with Princess Overbite?"

"No, Pete. I was with Edie."

"Your opulent wench from Connecticut?"

"Pennsylvania."

Peter scrunched his nostrils. His eyebrows danced luridly. "Did you give her a right roger up the old rumpty tumpty tum?"

"Hardly."

Peter laughed moronically. It didn't matter if you were discussing Chiang Kai-shek or the Gadsden Purchase. He'd always make the same crack and giggle like a simpleton.

"So, you finally whammed her?"

"Yep."

"You had sexual intercourse?"

"No. We discovered radium together."

"Does Edie give good head?"

"I don't know."

"You don't know?"

"No."

"What was she like in bed?"

"Great."

"How do you know, if you didn't get any head?"

"Jesus, Peter. What's with the Roland Kreisler? You're giving me the third degree."

"You're such a romantic, Douglas. You remind me of an old movie. Every time a chick appears, your string section goes up."

I spread grape jelly on my toast.

"Love is more than just sex, Peter."

"That's a laugh. So much *Sturm und Drang* to find the right girl, who, once you've got her, won't be right any more."

"When our minkies fail, romance is all we have."

Peter stretched out on his chair with a cigarette in his mouth and his thumbs in his garrison belt. Crossing his ankles, he snuffed, with dismissive condescension, "Romance? Have you checked the shelf life on romance?"

"Love is eternal. I think you're just being flip."

"A stiff prick has no Weltanschauung, Dougie. You're living proof."

Peter was quite the cad. Yet, he was easily hurt. One day, a big Italian kid named Del Santo saw Peter in the shower and said, "Hey, Fletcher. I didn't know you had such a small minky."

Peter went pale. He prided himself on his physique.

"I haven't the slightest idea what you're talking about."

"Ah, well," laughed the Italian. "The curse of the Irish."

It was a joke, but it devastated Peter. "Del Santo said that I have a munchkin minky."

I fought to keep a straight face.

"Why would he say that? *Why*?" Peter cradled his head in his hands. "Del Santo called me 'a pretty boy.' He said that pretty boys don't pack much in the meat department.'"

"You're always preening, Peter. You spend half the day in front of the mirror."

Peter stared at the floor with sad spaniel eyes. His lip quivered wildly.

"Fuck Del Santo. He's a greaseball from New Jersey," I said.

When Scott Fitzgerald thought he had a small minky, Ernest Hemingway took him to the Louvre and showed him the statues. But what could I do? Take Peter to the Smithsonian? The first thing you see there is that giant elephant.

CHAPTER 12

Meetings with Remarkable Messes

Finally my soul explodes and wisely she screams at me:
"Get me anywhere! Anywhere! Just so it's out of this world!"
—*Baudelaire*

PETER'S MINKY WAS SUBJECTED to more scrutiny than the Shroud of Turin. He thought nothing of coming in my room with a hand mirror and gazing at himself from all angles.

"Peter! My roommate is from Brooklyn. He's not gonna be happy when he finds you on his bed, ogling your dong."

"Be candid, Dougie. Does my dick look too small?"

"No. It looks about the same size as mine."

A look of panic came into Peter's eyes. He swore under his breath, and crossed himself. I felt like Jonathan Harker asking directions to Count Dracula's castle.

"What are you worried about, Pete? You can have any chick you want."

"Not any *chick*. Any *deb*. There's a big difference."

"Yeah. Debs have more money."

"Oh, Douglas. You truly are a babe in the woods. What on earth would I do with a debutante?"

"The same thing you do with other girls. Screw them till their heads explode."

"Puh-lease. I cannot abide tootsy girls. They have everything they want except sex. And they'll get that from the cabana boy."

"They'll need us to be their dates. To take them to parties."

"What? You mean, carry their gloves and shawls, like Lord Byron? Thank you very much, but, no thank you."

"Lord Byron was a lady's man, Peter. He was the *cavaliere servente* of Countess Teresa Guiccioli. She was the last great love of his life before he died in 1824 while trying to free the Greeks."

Peter eyed me coolly. He glanced outside my open window as youthful laughter wafted up from Dahlgren Chapel.

"Ah! That must be morning Mass."

Peter could drag himself to church in a drunken stupor.

"I never see you at Mass anymore," he chided wistfully.

"Small wonder. I'm a lapsed Episcopalian."

"I don't know what I'd do without my Catholic faith."

"I believe in God. Isn't that enough?"

Peter shivered. "No," he said fearfully, "not with all the horror abroad in the world."

I tried to placate him. "Remember what Swinburne said to Lucy Brown Rossetti? He said, 'My dear child, you must believe in God in spite of what the clergy tell you.'"

Peter knelt before my bed and began to pray. He began to cry, in choking little sobs. I tried to pray, too, but my mind was a jumble. I thought of everything sad that had happened.

First, there was the death of John Coltrane that summer. Then, my dog had to be put to sleep. Shep was the best pal I ever had. I take solace that he lived a full, happy life with a family that adored him. If they have border collies in heaven, Shep will be center stage, snapping at firecrackers and chasing firework helicopters. No dog ever had more fun on the Fourth of July than Shep. And if there are Elysian Fields, Shep will be bounding through them, putting joy in the heart of another little boy.

"Douglas," gasped Peter, "do you have a picture of the Pope that I might borrow?"

"Sorry. I'm fresh out of Pope pictures."

"I left mine at the Mayflower Hotel."

Peter groaned. He began to rummage through my fridge for a little hair of the dog.

"Pabst Blue *yuck*? Dear God. Nothing imported?"

"I have a bottle of Bordeaux."

"Does it have a name?"

"Bordeaux. I guess."

"Is it *appellation contrôlée*?"

"I'm not sure. I'm a TV baby, raised on Bosco."

"Who's the *négociant*?"

"Who's the what?"

Peter was hung over.

"Does it have a cork?"

"Beggars can't be choosers."

"Beggar? I get invited to a lot more parties than you, buddy boy."

I couldn't argue. Peter's good looks and princely manners made him a hit with the Washington hostesses of the day. I might land an invitation twice a week, while Peter had his choice of A-list affairs.

Party invitations were handled by Mrs. Hesketh and Mrs. Whipple, social dreadnoughts with Connecticut Avenue addresses. When you saw their stationery in your mailbox, you knew it was party time.

Black tie was the uniform of the day unless you were the deb's escort. Then you merited white tie. I never saw the Great Ghastly in a tux. He was far too flamboyant. Peter only wore white tie, and he cut a dashing figure with his smile and ranginess, like a young Ted Williams. I envied the spectacle Peter created among the foxiest girls as they vied for a whirl on the wax with the winsome one.

"I would take you to brunch, but I'm *sans sou*."

"You were going to quit drinking. You made a vow to 'The Desert Fox.' What were his words?"

Peter glared angrily. "Rommel said that 'Man must rid himself of his inner *Schweinhund*.'"

"I'm only quoting you, Peter. You... we promised to swear off.

Chill out. I'll take you to The Tombs for a taco."

"Good. So I won't have to kick your ass."

"Allah favors the compassionate."

"You've never seen my dukes in action. I'm no slouch in the fisticuffs department."

"Sure, Peter. If I'd lost my cool the other night at the Saudi embassy, you'd have been slunk meat."

Peter paled. He sat down heavily.

"I don't know what got into me, Dougie. I really don't."

Peter was upset, so I let it drop. But it was a psycho deal, nonetheless. Our Bedouin hosts had thrown a monster bash at the embassy, and everybody had a blast. When the party let out and I was getting in my car, a powerful hand grabbed me from behind by my cummerbund. The next thing I know I'm in a non-title bout with Peter on Massachusetts Avenue.

Happily, Peter's in dancing pumps and not getting much traction, so I let him wing away before I shot in for the single leg takedown. Brawlers don't fare well against wrestlers. True, wrestling is useless against multiple assailants, but in one-on-one confrontations, grappling is supreme. Let your man miss with his Sunday punch. Then take him to the deck and choke him out.

I worked in Georgetown bars and became adept at dealing with drunks. When you work till two or three in the morning, belligerent assholes are almost your stock-in-trade. Saloon work was a kick during the day because there were few drunks and you could lead a relatively normal life. But in barrooms, the big money was made at night, and that's when the real eight balls crawled out.

When I waited tables at The Apple Pie on M Street, drunks were my line of country. Friday and Saturday nights I drew Stiff Patrol. It was my job to chase down the stiffs who tried to beat out on their checks. Stiffs would have dinner upstairs and hoof it out the door while the dance floor was jumping downstairs. The stiffs weren't all street mutts, either. I bagged stiffs from every walk of life, or, I should say, every run of life, because they were usually hauling ass.

"All right, runt. I'm gonna waste you."

"You're drunk, Peter. Let's get in the car."

Peter cut a ridiculous figure as he circled me in his tailcoat outside the Saudi Arabian embassy.

"You've never fought a street fighter before."

"Oh, right. You grew up on the mean streets of Back Bay."

Fighting a pal is never as scary as fighting a stranger, especially nowadays when you've got some very bad hombres on some very bad drugs.

In a street fight, it's a good idea to land your most devastating technique right off the bat. Let them have it in the nuts before they go for a weapon. Forget that Caine on *Kung Fu* crap. Smash them over the head with a chair.

Cars were streaming out of the party and catching us in their headlights. I moved steadily backwards so I could lure Minky Boy onto the grass.

I didn't want to smack Petey in the puss because he was so drunk he didn't know what he was doing. Also, you can break your hand punching someone in the face. Hit them in the mouth, and you can get a nasty infection.

"Are you afraid yet, little man?"

"Sure. I feel like I'm being stalked by Charlie McCarthy."

Fuming, Peter came in, throwing haymakers from deep right field. "I'm going to thrash you within an inch of your life."

"What if I'm on the metric system?"

Nothing would deter Peter. His blood was up and so were his dukes. Normally, he was of a timid stripe, but the booze gave him Dutch courage. I tried not to laugh as he came at me with his John L. Sullivan brand of pugilism.

"Your ass is grass, MacKenzie."

"If you hurt me, I'll tell Peter Duchin."

"I don't care if you tell Peter Duchin."

"You will when he stops taking your song requests."

I got on my toes as Peter waded in, throwing shots with bad intent.

He had mustard on a right cross, but it was so telegraphed I could've blocked it in my sleep.

"Ha!" crowed Peter as he landed a glancing blow.

"You're really asking for it, scooter."

"Stand still and fight like a man."

Fighting in formal wear is surreal.

Finally, Peter got too close and I threw him to the ground. I wound up on my back, and he wound up on top of me.

I was in danger of being in the mounted position with a knee on each side of my body. From here he could've punched my face in, but I instinctively went into the guard. My legs shot up and cinched him so his blows fell short of my face.

I waited for Peter to get off balance and then flipped him into a reversal. I had him on all fours from behind with my left arm around his waist and my right hand gripping his right ankle.

"Unhand me this instant."

I rode Peter as he pitched forward onto his face.

"No way," I puffed. "Not until you stop fighting."

"The battle's not over, Uxbridge."

Peter was determined not to give up, and, in his effort to break free, ripped his tailcoat apart, dead center, up the middle.

"You beastly little wog," he cried at the top of his voice. "You've ruined my tuxedo. This is my new tailcoat that Mummy bought. In Savile Row. My clothes are bespoke. Yours are not."

"I have some spiffy duds," I said, wounded.

"Off the rack is off the rack," said Peter. "Your clothes don't fit. So you ruin mine. Look at my coat. Just look at it. What did I do to deserve this?"

"Well, for starters, you ruined my cummerbund."

I found my damaged waistband and showed it to Peter. "The little clasps are ruined. When you grabbed me from behind, you tore them out."

Peter looked contrite. "I hope it wasn't expensive."

"It's madras," I explained. "See. It matched my tie."

"Good God."

"It was a graduation gift from Miss Charlotte."

"*The* Miss Charlotte—of Foxcroft School?"

"I'm afraid so."

This piece of news rocked Peter. To him, the cummerbund was sacred. But I was pulling his leg. My actual graduation present from the legendary founder of Foxcroft School, Miss Charlotte Noland, was a silver money clip with St. Christopher on it.

"Miss Charlotte is right up there with Endicott Peabody."

"She is, indeed. She's Kate Hepburn's cousin."

"Douglas," said Peter, "I am truly sorry."

"Don't worry about it."

"Nobility obligates. Give me your cummerbund, and I'll see it's restored to new."

I gave the cummerbund to Peter, and in the whirl of freshman year, forgot about it. Some months later, I was borrowing a can of shoe polish when, to my chagrin, I found my cummerbund in Peter's shoe-shine kit.

"Revolution is not a dinner party. Wake up... wake up... up, up, up."

"I'm awake, Peter. Oh, by the way, I found my cummerbund."

"Cummerbund? You wear a Nehru jacket. What would you want with a cummerbund?"

"Nehru jacket? I don't have... any Nehru jacket."

"Rubbish, you don't. Right there. In that closet."

My heart sank as I had a sudden insight of how geeky I must have looked, dancing around in a Nehru jacket.

"I didn't buy that jacket, Peter. It's a rental. I swear. I can show you the receipt."

Suddenly, a look of alarm erased his smirk. He produced a calling card from his dressing gown pocket.

"I forgot to tell you. You're supposed to call Polly."

My heart raced. "When did she call?" I glided down the hall like a spirit.

The mundane scene of New North was transformed into an enchanted dreamland. I put a quarter in the wall phone and dialed a local number.

"Hello," answered a girlish voice.

"Polly, you angel. It's Doug."

A screech came over the line. It stunned me. *It was Edie.*

"Oh, Edie. I *knew* it was you. How's it going?"

"What did you do to my neck, you bastard? Donna had to rush me to the emergency room in the middle of the night."

"Could you call me back? We're having a fire drill, and I have to report to my muster station. Chop, chop. Toodle loo."

I hung up and ran back to my room to accost Peter. He was on Don's bed, inspecting the latest *Playboy.*

"That wasn't Polly, you pillock. It was Edie, and she lambasted me like a fishwife."

Peter was unruffled. He riffled through the magazine with an air of supreme unconcern.

"I can't keep your women straight," he said breezily.

"Get dressed. We gotta make tracks."

"We'll nosh somewhere posh," said Peter. "What about The Occidental? My treat."

This meant we were having burgs at Roy Rogers, on me.

"Let's go to Mama Ayesha's for an *arrack*," I said. "You can wear your *kaffiyeh* and denounce the Zionists."

"No," said Peter. "Let's go to the Rowdy Rooster."

"It's the last place on earth Edie would look," I said.

"Capital idea," said Peter. "Shorty should have my acid by now."

CHAPTER 13

Dial M for Mofo

I have lived for Art, for Love.
I have never hurt a living soul.
Lord? Ah, why do you repay me so?
—*Tosca*

PETER'S GREEN AUSTIN-HEALEY SPRITE jounced wildly down the cobble-stones of 34th Street before jostling onto the streetcar tracks of Old Georgetown.

When Woodrow Wilson was president, my father, Don, and his older brother, Burr MacKenzie rode the streetcar from their house on Ingomar Street to Central High School. Central High's most famous grad was J. Edgar Hoover, "who always got his man, but never a woman."

"WE'RE IN NO HURRY ON MY ACCOUNT!" I screamed.

Dancing on the edge of adhesion, Peter manhandled the skittery "Bug Eye" through a corner. Sawing at the Bakelite steering wheel like Tazio Nuvolari, he leaned from side to side, milking drama from every exertion.

I braced for impact as we nearly sideswiped a black Tolman Laundry truck.

"I have prettier hair than Doris Day," shouted Peter.

"WATCH THE ROAD, YOU FREAKING MANIAC."

"DON'T BE SUCH A PUSSY, MACKENZIE."

Riding with Peter was a hair-raiser.

We drove across Key Bridge and headed up Wilson Boulevard into North Arlington. When we came to Peoples Drugs, Peter turned in and switched off the motor.

"What are you doing?"

Peter gave me an arrogant smirk. He foppishly removed his Jim Clark driving gloves. "I am going to roll us a joint."

"You scared me. I thought we were putting the top up."

Putting the top up in a British roadster was a bore.

"This is some righteous weed, my little man."

"Where have I heard that before?"

Peter pulled out one of those honkie mofo rolling machines and rolled a malformed marijuana cigarette, using strawberry rolling papers.

"Is this pot any good?"

"Any good? This is pure Oaxacan gold grown from seeds handed down by a lost tribe of Aztec priests living in a cloud-shrouded Incan monastery in the Peruvian rain forest at the edge of an extinct volcano."

"Where'd you get it?"

"From this spade at Junior Hot Shoppes."

We blasted the entire doob. Nothing happened.

"Man," said Peter with a hip head bop, "this shit is *subtle*."

"I can't feel anything. We just blew an inert substance."

Peter exhaled, deflated. "Obviously, you've never smoked *zen pot* before."

———◆———

Located in a strip mall in Arlington off Wilson Boulevard, the Rowdy Rooster turned out to be a real dive. It was so dark, I half expected to see tube worms, if they turned on the lights.

"You'll love the atmosphere in here," said Peter. "It's cutting edge."

I peered at an *Olde Heurich Amber Lager* beer sign. It had strips of curly flypaper hanging from it.

"Holy lockjaw. It's not the Waldorf."

"Relax. No one's gonna murder you in broad daylight."

"That's what they told President Garfield."

I was about to scram when we were greeted by a rumpled old waiter with a dirty apron and a well-honed grin.

"Stump," croaked Peter. "How's it going?"

Stumpy was a weather-beaten relic with skin so leathery he could've been the torso portion of a shrunken head.

"So how's the world been treating you?" asked Peter.

"Shorty's been fucking me like a tired sheep," said Stumpy as he showed us to a table in front of the jukebox.

"The minute I come through the door, I knowed he had the DDTs."

Stumpy looked at Peter for sympathy. Then, he turned his sunken eyes on me.

"I'm Doug," I said cheerfully.

Stumpy glared at me like I was in town for a cult murder. Dick and Perry got a warmer welcome in Kansas.

"Stump," said Peter, "show Doug the plate in your head."

Stumpy stuck his skull in my face, and put my hand on it. "Feel that?"

Suddenly, I wasn't hungry any more.

"Yes. I feel it."

"I was doin' ninety on my Indian when I went and smacked a bridge abutment."

"You're lucky to be alive," I commiserated.

Peter broke out in a madhouse cackle.

"Stumpy has so many plates, he should pick out a China pattern."

"You had a tank slapper. What happened?"

"Some cager done a left turn in front of me. The same day I got my scoot out of the shop. What kin I git you young fellers?"

Peter composed himself and spoke preciously. Like a Junior Commodore of the Yacht Club.

"Let's see. I'll have a bacon, lettuce, and tomato on whole wheat toast with extra crispy bacon and only the center slices of tomato.

Oh, and Stumpy, advise the chef that I only want Heinz ketchup and Hellmann's mayonnaise, with no crusts on my toast."

"One BLT on toast," confirmed Stumpy in a rural twang.

"I'll have a hamburger, please," I said pleasantly.

"A hamburger?" repeated Stumpy, like I'd lapsed into a lost dialect.

"Medium rare, please. With extra onions."

"Okay. I reckon you know what you're doing."

Stumpy's jaw was set with grim resolve.

"Um… I think I'll have a BLT. Crusts and all."

"Ooh, baby," cooed Peter. "You swing."

"Now, what kin I git you young fellers to drink?"

"I'll have a Heineken's," said Peter sweetly.

"Pabst Blue Ribbon," I said.

"Breakfast of champions," chuckled Stumpy.

The moment Stumpy was out of earshot, I rounded on Peter. "Thanks for taking me to the Black Hole of Calcutta."

Peter lazily lit a cigarette. "Don't be such a snob."

Before I could reply, we were startled by the sounds of a wracking cough coming from the kitchen.

"Shorty," whispered Peter. "His bituminous days are catching up with him."

"Great. That sets the tone for fine dining."

Stumpy looked harried when he brought our beers.

"Shorty's sicker'n a shithouse rat."

"We're in no hurry, are we, Douglas?"

I braved a smile as Stumpy filled our ears with Shorty's medical update.

"Why doesn't he see a doctor?" asked Peter.

"He blowed his dough on a lady of the evening."

"You mean… a hooker?" asked Peter.

"My daddy used to say, 'If it flies, floats, or fucks…, you're better off with a rental.'" Stumpy cackled hoarsely.

"Y'all like the Redskins?"

"Sure," said Peter. "Pull up a chair."

"Don't mind if I do," said Stumpy.

Stumpy's cowpoke geniality charmed Peter. I was put off by the old guy when he sat down with the soles of his shoes facing us. You show folks the bottoms of your feet in Thailand and they'll put you off the bus.

"The Redskins got two quarterbacks and neither one can roll a watermelon down a hill."

"All I care about is beating Dallas," said Peter.

"Hey," I whispered, "I thought we were gonna cop."

LSD was legal in the summer of 1966. By October, Congress passed a law making its possession a misdemeanor.

"Come on, Peter. We're here to score. Not hang out with the Bog People."

"Food's up," chirped Stumpy as a little bell rang in the kitchen.

Our BLTs were delicious. We gobbled them up in no time flat. When there was nothing left on our plates but potato chips, I flagged Stumpy for the check.

"Go easy on this shit," said Stumpy as he slipped Peter a neatly folded, small, brown paper bag.

"Is it strong?" asked Peter expectantly.

Stumpy winked. "A little dab'll do ya."

"What's that mean?" I asked.

"Just don't do the whole shebang."

"HOT CHA CHA," jived Peter, snapping his fingers like a pseudo hepcat.

"Let's cut, man."

It was a groovy summer night in the District. In 1967, Washington was home to everyone from jazz great, Duke Ellington, to rock stars "Papa" John Phillips and Jim Morrison. D.C. in the Sixties was more than the Nation's Capital. It was our California.

"PUT YOUR WELLIE IN IT!"

Peter Fletcher hammered the throttle, and we rocketed through the city with the limey mill on full song. The more out of control we were, the more fun it was.

"You need a Sprite to attain the godhead."

"I know. Forty miles an hour and you're Fangio."

"WE'RE GONNA BE... ON LSD!" screamed Peter. We blasted back to school in the little roadster. The Sprite packed forty ponies from its tiny four-banger.

"SHE'LL DO EIGHTY, NO PROBLEM!" shouted Peter.

Peter's head was a blurred blonde flame all the way back to Georgetown. When he wasn't chasing fat stenographers and Howard Johnson's hostesses, Peter Fletcher was a cool hombre.

Once we were back on campus, he switched off the engine and threw the little bag in my lap. Carefully unwrapping the parcel, I pulled out something unexpected. It was, to my astonished eyes, nothing less than a bunch of cow manure.

CHAPTER 14

Prince Pussytoes Runs Amok

The everlasting universe of things flows through the mind.
—*Shelley*

"We just got burned."

"No way," protested Peter.

"Look for yourself. This is pure cowpie."

"They're magic mushrooms."

"Well, they're in it," I replied, bewildered.

"That's because they grow in it. Mushrooms are sacred. The Aztecs called them 'the flesh of the gods.'"

"Gee, I don't know, man."

"You can become William Blake, man."

"I don't want to become William Blake. I want to bonk hippie chicks, and they eat acid."

Peter lit a cigarette and exhaled impatiently.

"Don't you trust Shorty? You're paranoid."

"I'm afraid of amateur mycologists. And novice fugu chefs. Mushrooms can turn out to be toadstools. You play guinea pig, Pete. I'll take notes."

Peter bitched me out for not taking the mushrooms, but he didn't take them, either.

Mushrooms were the last thing on my mind when I got a letter from Polly Hay. She said she was coming to D.C. and fully intended to "give me what I wanted when we were in France." When I read those words, I yelped at the watercolor sky.

Peter was on crank and looking for pussy. He'd wasted the weekend, trying to pork a chubby chick he'd picked up at The Keg. She lived in Silver Spring with some other tattoo victims, and he spent most of the time driving up and down Georgia Avenue. I didn't care where he bestowed his affections, but I knew the speed was driving him nuts.

At first he started taking the stuff to cram for exams, and, then, as they say, it became a habit.

Peter and I popped Preludin to improve our grade point averages. Not only did we flunk every exam, I dashed off eight incoherent pages, answering only the first essay question of the American History midterm.

Peter had become such a yammering idiot that he never even made it into the exam building. I found him sprawled in the grass outside White-Gravenor Hall, having a chat with the earthworms.

Peter and I soon found ourselves shunned by our classmates, like evangelical lepers. But the speed had put us on such ego trips, we didn't notice.

Nothing is boring once the speed grabs hold. And anyone you encounter is your long-lost friend. I recall having expansive feelings for Sted Egley, our resident shlub.

I loathed the sight of Sted, and he loathed me. Calling him a dork overstated the case. Sted didn't have the *gravitas* to be a dork. That didn't stop me from cornering him inside Wisemiller's Market and talking his ear off. He was buying a donut when I buttonholed him with the business pages of *Time* magazine. Now, normally, I never read *Time*, and I hate business. But the demon speed had turned me into such a vacuous blowhole, I made Howard Cosell seem like Socrates.

Just when Sted Egley thought he'd effected a graceful exit, he ran smack into Peter. If I was the NERF version of tiresome twaddlers, Peter was the Louisville Slugger. You'd do a Hart Crane header into the

Potomac before you could endure what Peter had to say.

I couldn't crack a book without his background yap. When he wasn't yammering like a bag lady, he was drooped in my door, studying me like Jane Goodall. I tried to give him the shake by hiding in the library, but Riggs was more a time capsule than a modern library. Crammed in Healy Hall, the Riggs Library was so antiquated the Dead Sea Scrolls would've been catalogued under "Contemporary Fiction."

I lost track of Peter, now my new roommate, the next week. Then he popped up out of the blue in high spirits and new clothes.

"I've been all over Georgetown," he puffed. "And all I've seen are drunks, whores, junkies, and queers."

"If you think they're bad, you should see the sophomores."

"I meant downtown Georgetown," he chuckled.

Peter was too friendly. He had more up his sleeve than a Piaget watch.

"We're inseparable, Dougie. I want you to Boswell my Johnson."

"You keep your johnson to yourself."

He laughed a stage laugh. "Can we talk, heart to heart?"

I put aside my irregular French verbs. Taking an egg timer from my desk, I plopped it over so the white grains of sand began to fall in their measured cadence. "Okay. Start talking."

Peter quailed. He glared at my sandglass like it was a menacing queen. "I feel like I'm on *Beat the Clock*."

I eyed him coldly. Molotov didn't give Hitler a meaner scowl.

"Guess what? I stopped doing speed. And I stayed up all night reading your proddy dog Bible. Man, that King James cat could write."

"Fine. Listen, I have a lot of homework, and I need to do it now because Polly's coming to town."

"Polly? The chick with the Kabuki makeup?"

"You should see her now. She looks like Grace Kelly."

"You mean, Emmett Kelly."

"Don't disrespect the woman I love."

"I need a ride to the doctor, Dougie, old pal."

"What's wrong with the Green Weenie?"

"Won't start. I think it's the solenoid."

Peter shrugged. He had the mechanical aptitude of a house finch.

"When's your appointment?"

"In an hour."

"Crazy. Let's book."

It was a boisterous chamber of commerce day, with frilly clouds galore. The Vette was right where I left it. We put the top down.

"Let's do a chick check. This could be the last day for miniskirts."

Side pipes burbled as we cruised East Campus, admiring the school 'make-out squad.' I turned up the radio so we could hear "Go Where You Wanna Go."

"They call me the 'Tar Baby of Love,'" swaggered Peter languidly. "Women can't keep their hands off me."

We came to a stop. "Which way, Tar Baby?"

"One more spin around the block," he said with his Tyrolean hat cocked at a jaunty angle.

"WHOA! CHECK THE NUMBER COMING OUT OF TEHAAN'S!"

"Where?"

"With the big sweater muffins. In the Campbell Plaid."

I was in the scan mode when I locked eyes with our universally reviled Dean of Men, Regis M. Klumph. My heart sank as I slumped down, trying to hide.

"We're fucked. Klumph gave us the evil eye. Don't turn around," I warned.

So what does Peter do? He turns around and gapes at the dean with a look of abject terror.

"I TOLD YOU NOT TO TURN AROUND!"

"He didn't notice us," lied Peter.

"Oh, sure. What's conspicuous about a red Corvette?"

"Klumphy only busts boozers at polo matches. We're cool."

"Yeah. Straight from the fridge, dad."

I turned onto Wisconsin and headed downhill to K Street. At K, I hung a louie at Chadwick's and gassed it hard past The Bayou.

"Where's your croaker?"

"14th and U," answered Peter blandly.

"That's Indian country."

"It can be a little dicey. But only at night."

The Vette makes its presence known. It lumbers down 14th Street, garnering looks from the pimps, hookers, winos, and dope peddlers. Back then, 14th Street was a thriving hive of jive with dirty book stores, peep shows, and X-rated movies galore. Then, some Do Rights came along and fucked it up.

On a recent nostalgia tour I cruised down Chapin Street. Chapin used to be Reefer Central. Now the Blunt boys have packed in. I'm not ashamed to say I got a little misty when I couldn't find my amigos. The cats weren't jumpin' and jivin' on the corner. Same story on 11th and O. Now, everywhere you look, you see Tinkertoy townhouses and trendy condos. The situation has gotten so bad, you can't find a decent criminal anymore.

"Ditch the Hitler hat, Petey."

"Why should I?"

"Bro's don't need to see whitey with a shaving brush on his head."

Peter doffed his ofay sky and chucked it behind the seat. "Turn right, man. Park on Newton."

Dr. Woolton's medical practice was conveniently located on a major heroin corridor. Peter was unfazed. Life for him was a dogleg par four.

"Will my car be safe?"

"Chipper dipper."

"Shouldn't we put the top up?"

"Why? It's a beautiful day."

D.C. was holy before crack hit town. I could park anywhere, with the top down and eight track tapes in plain view. No one touched a thing. The old-time shmeckers had class.

"We should have worn our blue blazers."

"We're not dropping in on Kate Hepburn."

Peter sauntered up the short flight of stairs to the doctor's office and rang the bell. A tall, reedy Negro in a yellow jumpsuit let us in. He showed us to a waiting room downstairs and returned to his post upstairs, where he sat on a folding metal chair.

"That's 'Slim,'" said Peter. "He's the receptionist."

"You mean, the bouncer?"

Slim was easygoing. He nipped peach brandy from a brown paper bag while the doctor saw patients.

"I was here the day Slim took a header down the stairs."

"Bummer."

Dr. Woolton's office was an old Victorian heap that had been Balkanized like Ralph Richardson's house in *Dr. Zhivago*. The waiting room was on your immediate right as you entered the building.

"Oh, shite," cried Peter. "It's chockablock."

To our chagrin, the room was wall-to-wall with white hippie hairheads. Dr. Woolton's practice was on its last leg, or limited exclusively to speed freaks.

"Yikes. It looks like the green room for the Bataan Death March."

Waiting patients gave us darting looks as they yammered at monkey-house noise levels. Skeletal arms floated like anemones. Everywhere you looked, magazines fluttered on bony knees that churned like valve tappets.

"Shiver me timbers. Pictures of matchstick men."

"Be cool," Peter advised me with jive wrist action. "You dig?"

"Yes. Thank you, Captain Hip."

I followed as we waded through the mob to two metal chairs in the back of the waiting room. I wondered how rail-thin geeks get speed, and Peter informed me that they feign narcolepsy and bus in from the suburbs with their medical histories in hand.

"Dr. Woolton is Willie Mosconi with a pen. He writes so many scripts, one arm is bigger than the other."

Another carload of hyper-animated hipsters spilled into the office. The waiting room was a madhouse. An elderly black woman bustled in wearing a wig that looked like a sea urchin.

"NO MORE LONG-HAIRED WHITE BOYS!" she screamed, barring the door.

Pandemonium peaked and, then, gradually, subsided. Vans were heard starting up and noisily driving off.

"Damn dope fiends," declared Peter. "They ruin it for everybody."

I tried to read a magazine, but Peter wouldn't leave me alone. He kept bugging me by reading over my shoulder and prompting me to turn the page.

"If you hit the doc after me, we double our score."

"I'm not hitting up your croaker, man. No way."

Peter's eyes burned me like a heretic.

"Why the hell not?"

"I'm not doing any more speed, Peter. Polly's coming to town, and I don't need my dick looking like Tom Thumb's Arctic Adventure. I never said I was seeing the doctor."

Peter was miffed. "You're buddy fucking your old amigo? Over a piece of tail? Oh, fine. Wait until the chips are down, then, double-cross me."

"This place is a zoo. I've wasted two hours. With a term paper due."

"You got to read *Ebony* magazine. You've been having fun."

Peter shook his head in disbelief. He hit me with the South American waif look.

"I can't handle uppers. I manic out on Nescafé."

"One lousy Preludin script for your old college chum."

I gave in and trudged up the stairs to the doctor's office. Slim had a transistor radio welded to his ear. I recognized Eddie Kendricks' falsetto: "Fee Fie Fo Fum. Look Out, Baby 'Cause Here I Come."

Slim held up a hand for me to wait. I leaned there as one Motown tune segued into another. I could hear the doctor behind the closed door.

"PRELUDIN!" crowed Dr. Woolton. "That's a narcotic. And I don't prescribe it."

It was time to see the doctor. I took a deep breath and breezed through the door with a big carhop smile.

Doctor Woolton was a blinky old catfish in a cheesy blue suit.

"Well, now. Howdy do, there? How are you?" he asked in a Delta drawl.

Some doctors have a cloak of moral steadfastness so you can't tell they are croakers. Not Woolton. He copped to croaker from the jump.

"Have a seat," he said pleasantly. "Office visits are five dollars. If I have to get my prescription pad, it's fifteen."

I found a chair amid the pagodas of medical files that had claimed every available surface.

"Mighty fine day, isn't it? Yes, sir. Mighty fine. Mighty fine."

"It's perfect weather for chucking the old pigskin," I laughed.

Doc Woolton considered me with kind eyes as I laid down the routine. "That's right. It's gridiron weather. I know it is. Yes, it is. Sho' nuff."

If I stayed cool and didn't cop to the Torso Murders, I'd get a prescription for something.

We made small talk, and the good doctor was the soul of congeniality. You could say anything, and he fell all over himself, agreeing with you.

"Dr. Woolton, did you hear the news? Giant atomic hedgehogs have kidnapped Lady Bird. They're holding her for ransom at the bottom of a uranium mine."

"They did? I heard about that. They sure did. I knew they would. Yes, indeedy. They sure did. Isn't that somethin'?"

And Doc Woolton was not without humor. He would slap his knee and beg for mercy as we derided the follies of man and dog. Stick to the blacksnake stories—the homespun yarns of the honeysuckle South, and he'd jelly over with mirth. Only when you broached the subject of drugs would he appear to age before your eyes. And if you were brazen enough to mention Preludin? His spindly limbs would jerk in a frisson of protest—the way a rabbit's do when you clip its toenails.

"Preludin!" he'd sputter in the timeworn way. "That's a narcotic, and I don't prescribe it."

Peter was smooth. He could make the doctor croak like a spring peeper.

"But, Dr. Woolton," Peter would say, "Dr. Rosenbaum...."

Once they were in the ritual bartering phase, when Dr. Woolton would shout, "WHAT DO YOU WANT?" Peter cannily upped the ante by throwing out the name of his chimerical Jewish doctor who was providing him with fabulous medication.

"Dr. Rosenbaum has me on a rolling IV of morphine."

"MORPHINE IS A NARCOTIC, AND I DON'T PRESCRIBE IT!"

Thus, my roommate went through a declension of deadly drugs until he reached Preludin, which, by now, the good doctor was ready to prescribe.

"WHAT DID YOU GET?" snarled Peter in the grip of some misguided rage.

"Placidyls."

"You didn't? You asshole. You know who uses Placidyls? Housewives."

"That's what he gave me."

"Did you tell him you were in the Lion's Club?"

"The Lion's Club?"

"I told you to tell him you were in the Lion's Club. You've got to come across as civic-minded. You need an upright image. Croakers are like chicks. They want you to paint them a sunny picture. Even if it's jive. It's expected."

"I was a Cub Scout. I guess I could've mentioned that."

"Placidyls are putrid. They permeate your body with a piny smell, like those little Christmas candles. Gimme your script."

"How come?"

Peter brooded as though this was a perceived slight. He was so unpredictable. One second he was your pal, the next suffused with anger.

"Just give it to me. You won't be able to bust it, anyway. Woolton's scripts are a joke. Unless you know the right drug store."

"What did he give you?"

"Don't be a tapeworm, MacKenzie."

"Here. Take it. I'll stick with Bass Ale."

Peter snatched the script. He trotted off down a litter-strewn alley and left me standing there.

"HOW DO I GET BACK ON M STREET?" I shouted after him.

"Follow the trolley car tracks, man."

The trolley tracks were gone. Or they led nowhere.

Nearer My Bod to Thee

Before me I saw a tombstone. I heard a glowworm, big as
a house, say to me: "I will give you the light you need."
—— *Le Comte de Lautréamont, Les Chants de Maldoror*

"**DOUG?**"

"Polly!"

"Wow. I can't believe it's really you."

"Where are you?"

"Crashing at a friend's. Near American University."

I froze.

"Who is he?"

Polly laughed easily on the phone. Too easily. She had that run-on, dieseling laugh prevalent among acid heads.

"*She* is an old friend. Do you know how to get to A.U.?"

"Sure. Just zip up Nebraska Avenue."

'We can stay in bed all day. We don't even have to eat. We can do *anything*. Use your imagination."

Yipes! I was using my imagination. I was trying to come up with someone who would take my busboy shift at Clyde's. I settled on Tom Costello.

"Dougie, I need to tell you something. I was in a terrible accident. I was on a green mare, and she balked at a jump. I sailed over her neck and landed on my head."

"Bummer."

"Doug, I broke my neck."

"Jesus. You were just out hacking and..."

"No, I was riding to hounds."

"But you're okay, now?"

"I'm fine, except I don't have any teeth."

I tried to picture Polly without teeth. It was horrible at first. Then I started to visualize some scream-and-cream gum action.

"Doug? Are you still there?"

Poor Polly. Jeez. She could be on crutches. Or in a wheelchair. Or in an iron lung. I'd never given much thought to bonking the disabled, but now I was suddenly at ease with the idea.

"Are you ambulatory?"

"I was in the hospital for six months, but I'm fine, now."

"Did you get dentures?"

"Why would I need dentures?"

"Don't they include prosthetic choppers with cosmetic surgery?"

"I didn't get a nose job, Dougie. I broke my neck."

"But you still hate the French?"

"With a passion."

I spruced myself up, threw on some Old Spice, and jumped into the Plastic Pig. Threading my way through campus traffic, I drove past McDonough Gym and whistled out the back exit with pedal to the metal. The raised-letter Goodyears screamed as I dumped the clutch and laid rubber in twin black streaks on Reservoir Road.

I hung a right onto Nebraska Avenue and gunned it past American University. I was meeting Dream Cakes at a bookstore in Tenleytown on the upper part of Wisconsin.

The bookstore wasn't crowded, but I didn't see Polly. I did see a sweet little item in a beret, and a white Oxford shirt with the top buttons unbuttoned. For slacks, she wore revealing blue tights that highlighted her undies.

"Doug? Hi. It's me."

It was Polly's voice, but this chick had short hair and was almost waiflike.

"Polly? Wow, I didn't recognize you."

Before I could say more, she kissed me, lustily, longingly. Her coat was festooned with colorful novelty buttons. One said, "FUCK THE REAL WORLD—I'M AN ARTIST."

"I'm lucky to be alive, Doug. I was given the last rites."

She smiled ruefully. She had all of her teeth.

"Why'd you tell me you didn't have any teeth?"

"I said I didn't have any 'teats.'"

"You look great. I expected you to look horrible."

"And you showed up, anyway. That's reassuring."

"I dig your outfit. It's so pop culture."

"I was afraid to come, Doug. I'm not the girl you fell in love with."

"What girl was that?"

"Wait till you see me with my shirt off."

I could feel my blood coursing in the familiar way.

"Why are you dressed like that?"

Polly smiled her gala smile. "*Panache.* Do you remember Berlin? Berlin was an island of democracy fighting for survival in a sea of communism. John Kennedy stood before a huge crowd of Berliners and said, in very bad German, '*Ich bin ein Berliner,*' which means, 'I'm a jelly donut.' Naturally the crowd laughed. What President Kennedy meant to say was, '*Ich bin Berliner,*'' or 'I'm a Berliner.' But the gaffe didn't hurt him. Do you know why?"

"Because he was a glazed donut?"

"Because he had *panache.* He shored up the spirit of the freedom-loving Germans by declaring he was one of them. He assured them in their darkest hour that the West was behind them. John Fitzgerald Kennedy was the finest leader this country has produced.

"I want to do something for humanity," Polly declared, pounding her palm with her fist. "I want to join VISTA and the Peace Corps. I want to help the migrant farm workers. I'm going to work for Robert Kennedy. He's our only viable peace candidate, and he'll help the Negroes."

"They wouldn't let me in the Peace Corps."

"Why not?"

"They won't let you in the Peace Corps if you've been in military school. They're afraid I'd go to one of their banana republics and stage a coup."

"Well, what do you want to do, Doug? You have to decide."

"Oh, I know what I want to do. I want to blow the doors off a rat motor Chevelle. I want to beat a 289 Mustang's butt all over the place."

I was half joking, but Polly seemed disturbed by this information. I could tell she was deadly serious about politics, and that could spell trouble for me and Tadge. We might have to listen to a lot of Joan Baez records.

I thought about JFK as we strolled down the street to where Polly was staying. Just before Oswald's bullets struck our wonderful President, Nellie Connally put the whammy on him with: "You can't say that Dallas doesn't love you, Mr. President."

No woman incited lust in me like Polly Hay. She was full-service, sinfully delicious, and I found her light as a feather as I carried her into the bedroom and tossed her on the bed.

"Yikes," she cried as I tore off her clothes.

"What's wrong?"

"Can I pee before you ravage me?"

"Sure."

Polly skinned it down to her creature features and stood before me with a sad look on her face.

"This is what's left of me," she said solemnly.

She was so beautiful naked, I thought my heart would stop.

Polly hiked into the jakes and straddled the hopper. There was no bathroom door, but she wasn't in the least bit modest.

I heard the sound of plumbing and marveled at Polly's nakedness as she crossed the room. In those days American movies never showed any nudity. That's why I loved French movies. Bare breasts popped up everywhere. Even in detective movies.

Polly issued a giddy laugh and capered, naked, onto the bed.

"What are you smiling about?" she asked.

"I was thinking how phony it is in the movies when nude women get out of bed and drag all the covers off with them out of some misguided sense of modesty," I said.

"They do that because of the censors. You can't have anything about sex unless there's a doctor in a white coat at the beginning of the film. He sits behind a card table and spouts claptrap about the movie's socially responsible ramifications. When all you came to see was Jayne Mansfield naked."

"We're so repressed. In Victorian England it was improper to say 'leg.' It was only polite to say 'limb.' The Victorians were so paranoid they actually dressed up piano legs out of fear the men might become aroused."

"Put on a record," Polly said. "I want to get high."

I chose a Louis Armstrong album. She chafed at my selection.

"You don't want to hear Pops sing 'Hello Dolly'?"

"Put on Vanilla Fudge."

"That's the name of a group?"

Polly sighed as I perused the album cover. Vanilla Fudge looked like British Invasion wannabes in ill-fitting mod outfits.

"Which side would you like to hear?"

Polly scurried around the loft, looking for a candle. There was a jack-o'-lantern in the window, but she passed it up for a candle in a Mateus bottle.

"Oh, how Greenwich Village."

We sat on the rug and blew the best grass I'd ever had. Polly's Columbian was bright gold with fat, wooden seeds.

"This is righteous lumbo."

Vanilla Fudge rocked. Their innovative cover of "You Keep Me Hangin' On" was just killin'. I slipped into a dream sequence and saw myself as a child finding a joyful toad in my mother's garden. The candle and the music fused into Murano magic. In the flickering light Polly transformed into a high priestess.

"Wow. This is just like that scene in *Steppenwolf*."

"In what?"

"In the novel, *Steppenwolf*? When Harry gets turned on? Don't tell me you haven't read it."

"I read the *Reader's Digest* condensed version."

"You've never read Hermann Hesse?"

Polly's voice had a caustic edge. I could feel my manhood going through a Veg-O-Matic.

"Is it a new book?"

"It came out in 1927. Hermann Hesse only won the Nobel Prize for literature, Douglas."

"Oh."

"Well, what's your favorite book?"

It was more an accusation than a question.

"Uh... I guess I really enjoyed reading *Big Red*."

I was zonked. The only other book I could think of was *Thirty Seconds Over Tokyo*.

"*Big Red*? What's it about? Panama red?"

"Actually, it's about an Irish setter."

Polly laughed mockingly. "An Irish setter? You're joking?"

"It's a terrific book. You should read it."

"That is so lame. You probably liked *Lad, A Dog*."

Now Polly was Lady Sneerwell.

"I loved all the Albert Payson Terhune books," I said.

Polly's derisive cackle made my hair stand on end.

"What do they have you reading at Georgetown?"

"*The Ordeal of Richard Feverel*."

"Do you like it?"

"I like you."

I grabbed Polly and kissed her deeply. Then, I threw her on her back and pinned her there. Her literary pretensions were a memory as I gave her honey pot the 'Winnie the Pooh' treatment.

"My turn," said Polly in a husky voice.

Suddenly sharp teeth clamped down on The Tadge.

"Youch. Easy with the organ grinding. That hurts."

"Am I being too rough?"

"No. I like lacerations and contusions. Sweetheart. Take it easy. Two years ago, you were wearing pastel sweaters with your monogram on them."

"We had fun in Bayonne. And Lourdes."

"We did."

Polly sighed. Her eyes welled with tears. "You don't know what it's like to nearly die."

"I do, Polly. I got caught in a riptide, swimming off the coast of France. I was on the verge of drowning when some French guys in a motorboat spotted me and saved my life. Rip currents are drowning machines. Never fight the current. Swim parallel to the shore."

"Bummer," Polly said.

She lay back, affording me the best view in a boy's life.

Making it with Polly was kiddie car fun. She was so hot I felt like Yves Montand.

Afterwards, we lay together as rain pattered on the roof.

"'You and me and rain on the roof,'" Polly sang gaily.

I was drifting off when she gave me a shake.

"Doan you poop out, Mandingo. They's cotton left to pick."

"I's a comin', Miss Polly."

CHAPTER 16

Tripping with Sir Yack Yack Yack

Marijuana... Exhibit A.

—Jerry Garcia, Woodstock, 1969

POLLY AND I SPENT A LEISURELY MORNING reading the paper. The news was not good.

"I'm sick of Vietnam," she said. "We're committing war crimes to fatten up corporate America. LBJ's rotten cronies."

"We have to destroy it in order to save it."

"That's Orwellian, Douglas."

"But what about the domino theory?"

"That's rubbish disseminated by money-grubbing warmongers."

"We could get ripped on mimosas. Or Bloody Marys."

"You can't stick your head in the sand forever. Have you ever done anything political?" asked Polly.

"I was captain of the Hill School debating team in 1960."

Polly was exuberant. "You were for Jack Kennedy?"

"I was for Nixon."

"Nixon? You brain-dead little brown shirt."

"I was parroting my father. I was only twelve."

"Nixon?" she growled. "Oh, man. I just made it with Himmler."

Polly'd struck a nerve. It was hard being apolitical during the Sixties. But there I was, a little hedonist.

"Did you ever march for civil rights?" she asked.

"I marched in the Apple Blossom Parade with the RMA drill team."

In 1970, I integrated the lunch room at the Tolman Laundry. But it wasn't political. My best friend and co-worker was a fat black kid who cracked me up.

"Let's go into Georgetown. And have brunch," I said.

It was raining, so we made a mad dash for the car.

"Where are we going, Dougie?"

I considered an elegant eatery called The Guards. But Polly was wearing the Symbionese Liberation Army fall collection: red beret, army jacket, tiger cammies and jump boots.

"What about La Niçoise? And caviar omelettes? The owner, Jean-Louis Martin, is a buddy of mine."

"I don't need to see any frogs while I'm eating," groused Polly.

"The waiters are on roller skates. They blur by. Think of yummy eggs—omelettes with Beluga caviar, red onions, dill, and sour cream."

Just as we fishtailed onto Wisconsin, some clown in a GTO tried to get a run on the Pig. I downshifted, leaving him in the dust.

"Color me gone."

"Color you nuts," shrieked Polly. "Your car is just like you."

"How's that?"

"The Vette wanted to bonk that GTO."

"The 'Pig'? No way. I raised him better than that."

"I think exhausts are mating calls. Why else would someone want a Harley?"

I switched off the windshield wipers as we raced down Wisconsin Avenue, passing Sidwell Friends School.

Polly smiled and took out her compact.

"Let's burn a number, then, munch out deluxe," I said.

She looked hesitant.

"This is not what I'd call 'daytime pot,' Dougie."

"Big deal," I said naively. "How stoned could we get?"

Polly laughed her dieseling laugh.

"Turning on," she said, clicking her Zippo.

We watched in awe as the morning sun broke through the clouds and lit up Georgetown.

Polly fumbled with the radio dial and found Jefferson Airplane. Their sexpot lead singer, Grace Slick, was belting out "Somebody To Love."

Suddenly, we burst out laughing and couldn't stop.

"Whoa! Scope the pumpkins in that window. What's goin' on?"

"It's Halloween, Polly."

"Far out. What are you doin'?"

"Looking for a parking space."

"I can dig where you're coming from. It's like... so Samuel Beckett. I mean like the whole groove smacks of the existential. We can free associate on a cellular level. But it's the quantum physics that hits you over the head."

I was ready to hit her over the head.

I parked and we started walking down Wisconsin.

"Far out, man. Let's go in and groove on the trippy posters."

Halfway through the door of the Commander Salamander novelty store, I caught Polly's arm and dragged her back onto Wisconsin Avenue.

"Let's eat. Then, we can pipe the head shops."

"No frog bistros. I hate the uppity varmints."

"Hey, don't knock the French. They invented pornography."

I took Polly to Nathan's instead. Nathan's was an upscale lushing crib with great Northern Italian cuisine.

I asked for Booth 26, an intimate table in the back, and prime seating for a hot date.

Polly and I sat, stoned and slack-jawed as the waiters stumbled by, like Stepford wives.

"How do you get a waiter in an Italian restaurant?"

Polly was losing her patience.

"You can say 'senta,' which means 'hear me.' Or simply 'cameriere, per favore.'"

Polly jammed two fingers in her mouth and whistled.

"HEY," she barked. "BRING US SOME MENUS."

This prompted speedy service, but I wanted to crawl under the table. We were hungrily munching our breadsticks, when Peter Fletcher flaked through the door.

"Who is that attractive young man?" asked Polly.

Pete Fletcher was in last night's evening wear and, *horribile visu*, sporting a cane.

"It's Peter. Hide! Before he sees us."

Polly looked up as Peter squinted, searching the dining room. I tried hiding behind my menu.

"DOUGLAS, OLD MATE!"

Oh, sod.

"*ALTER JUNGE!*"

Oh, *Scheisse*.

"I see you, you little rodent."

"Pete. I didn't see you come in," I lied.

Peter flashed a Pepsodent smile. He fluttered over, like an art deco moth.

"AND WHO IS THIS RAVISHING CREATURE?"

For a world-weary sophisticate, Peter's moves were strictly five-and-dime.

"Polly, I'd like you to meet..."

"*Enchanté*," crowed Peter.

Sir Giles Overreach was already smooching Polly's arm, up to the elbow.

"Watch the slobber. Her watch isn't waterproof."

"Douglas, Janet Alexander was asking about you."

"I'm glad to hear it."

"He has a stable of Madeira girls at his beck and call."

"They're friends, Peter. Something you wouldn't understand."

Polly gazed moonily at Peter. Her eyes were like tiles embedded in cement.

"Won't you ask Peter to join us?"

Body blow. I wanted Peter at our table like I wanted to be shipwrecked with a Jehovah's Witness.

"Yes, Peter. Won't you join us?"

"Only for a minute," deigned Peter. "Then, I must nip off for the opening chukker."

"You play polo?" asked Polly, all gaga.

"Ripping good game, I must say."

"But it's so violent," cooed Polly.

Peter scavenged our dinner rolls. His teeth clacked like castanets.

"I try to stay fit," he stated resolutely.

The only workout Peter got was bouncing checks.

"Mind if I order the wine?" he said.

"Get a *Chateau Pétrus*," said Polly. "I like the '63."

"The '63s were filthy. Rainy summer. Rotten harvest. In a Pomerol, I should think, a '52."

"Let's not stint our guest," I said. "Order up a '45. And take out a second mortgage on 'Tara'."

"They don't even have a '28," sniffed Peter.

"A '28 would be boo coup bucks," said Polly.

"Diner's card will cover it," Peter laughed.

"Your Diner's card is deader than King Tut."

"Polly, order Douglas a Shirley Temple. Have the waiter bring a high chair."

"You have some nerve. First, you crash our table. Then, you commandeer our wine list. You know, you really are a swine."

Peter frowned and flagged down a waiter.

"Would you bring me a French 75? And the Chilean sea bass. No. No, just the drink."

He took out an English Oval and tapped it fastidiously on his silver cigarette case.

"Douglas. While you were feathering your love nest, I was in a bustle, obtaining some LSD."

"Get outta here. Where would you find any acid?"

"An old street associate."

"Is this the one who sold you the zen pot?"

Peter smoked with a cool detachment. He *did* have some LSD.

"It's not easy being an ambassador's son," announced Peter morosely.

Polly slurped up her soup with ravening pleasure. "It dang sure beats slingin' fries in a paper hat."

"Is that what you people do on Catfish Row?"

"I'm from South Carolina."

"Oh, really," said Peter. "By choice?"

Peter glowered. He wanted to impress Polly with his poor-little-rich-boy saga of being spirited from palace to palace, but she wasn't biting. She cared more about "Northern Dancer" and Churchill Downs than what the jet set was up to.

"Where did you find her? When they drained the swamp?"

"When they filled it," said Polly. "I floated up, clinging to your mother."

"If Mummy floats, it's at Bath and Tennis."

"Well, maybe they should clean the tub."

I watched Peter age before my very eyes.

"Why don't you show us the acid?" I said.

"Abracadabra," said Peter.

"LSD-25," croaked Polly in a W. C. Fields voice.

Four "blue smears" were nestled in Peter's outstretched palm.

"Be my guest," said Peter.

Polly ate the acid like it was a dinner mint. Peter followed suit. Now it was down to me.

"What about our fettuccine Alfredo? Shouldn't I titrate?" I asked apprehensively.

"You mean do half? You wouldn't get off."

"Could I eat first?"

I took a tab of acid and swallowed it neatly.

"You're in for it now," laughed Peter.

"What do you mean?" I asked with alarm.

"You both just did a four-way tab."

"Peter's not too swift when it comes to copping."

Polly was crushed. "You mean, I might not get off?"

"Peter's scored enough placebos to do a double-blind study."

"It might not be acid?"

"I wouldn't pin my hopes too high."

If we did start to trip, I had to stay on my toes. I had to make sure that Peter didn't sidetrack us into an imbroglio of social climbers and polo poofters.

"We should find a mellow place to trip. I don't want to be stumbling around like Bette Davis in *Dark Victory*," I said.

"I love stumbling around," said Polly. "It's more fun to see where the day takes you. I say we give ourselves up to the trades like the Flying Dutchman."

"I have a cool friend who could be our trip guide. He has a big room in New South."

"My sister is at Bennington. Her room puts our hovels to shame."

"My brother goes to Boston University," said Polly. "His room makes Bennington seem like a doss house."

"I say we get *The Tibetan Book of the Dead* and have my friend Clark Gribbet read us the juicy parts while we undergo ego death," said Peter.

"Barf," said Polly. "I'd rather have Colonel Mustard beat me with a candlestick."

"Pay the check, Douglas. Then, we'll nip round to see Clark."

"Who?" I asked.

Peter rolled his eyes and bore down on me with withering disdain.

"Clark Wentley Gribbet the Fourth. You know, 'Gobbler.'"

"Doesn't ring a bell."

Peter folded his napkin. "Someone needs to brush up on his Cleveland Amory."

"The only bloodlines worth knowing are horses," said Polly.

Peter shot me a reproachful look.

"Where did you pick up this albatross?" he whispered.

I got a bracing dose of daylight when we breezed out the door. It was that feeling you get when you leave the theatre after the matinée.

"Whoa!" cried Polly. "Scope the gold dome on that bank."

Peter led the way through Georgetown in a huff. He cut a chic figure with his cane as we paused to knock on Clark Gribbet's door. Clark had his own townhouse on P Street—pretty impressive for a lowly undergrad.

"Doesn't Pete look like Jeremy Brett in *My Fair Lady*?"

"He looks like Mr. Peanut," said Polly.

"He's been up all night. He's done in."

"Wait till he starts tripping. Then, we'll ditch him."

Peter rapped purposefully with the head of his cane on Clark's front door. No answer.

"That's odd. I cannot imagine where Clark might be."

This was not a propitious beginning for a first acid trip. We'd only dropped a half hour ago, and already it was bad vibes from Itchy Coo Park.

We turned away, and headed for Georgetown campus.

Peter and Polly fell mute. They lumbered along with sullen faces.

Then, the mood changed completely. We came upon something so hilarious it bonded us in mirth.

The statue of the Most Reverend John Carroll, first Archbishop of Baltimore and the founder of Georgetown University, had a giant pumpkin on his head.

This was the funniest thing we'd ever seen, and we all fell on the lawn together, howling with laughter. Poor Father Carroll had served as a Pasquino over the years. Look under his chair and you'll see the stone stack of books that was added to his statue to prevent student chamber pots from being placed there.

"Let's get Clark," shouted Peter. "He will die when he sees this."

We headed back to Clark's in a mad dash. In the throes of bedlamite laughter, we kicked, pummeled, and pounded on his door in a frenzy.

Finally, the door opened, and a plump figure peered out. It was Clark, and he wanted to see us like a clown car of escaped lunatics.

"Clark, old sport! Did we wake you?"

"As a matter of fact," he said groggily, "you did."

"Well, snap to. Make hay while the sun shines."

Clark was a walking pork chop. And a ringer for Hermann Goering.

"I was up all night," he said woozily.

"WHAT WERE YA DOIN'? BANGIN' BEAVER?"

Clark blinked at Polly.

"I was plotting azimuths and glide ratios. Rocket trajectories."

"WELL, WE JUST TOOK LSD."

Clark flashed a nebbishy smile. "So, you're exploring inner space?"

Polly nodded like Harpo. Her pupils were on high beam.

"Clark's our resident mad scientist. He's the only freshman to win the Goddard prize."

"Oh, now I'm Wernher Von Braun. At Peenemünde."

"Man," said Polly. "Talking to you is like talking to a textbook."

Peter cackled dementedly. "Father Carroll is Cinderella. Or he was. Now he's a pumpkin."

Clark tossed his forelock abstractedly. "What?"

Peter giggled. We all tittered like cartoon mice.

"FATHER CARROLL HAS A NEW HEAD, AND IT'S A PUMPKIN."

We howled until our maniacal merriment filled Clark's foyer like the shrieking souls of the damned. We were such idiots I expected Clark to chuck us out forthwith. Instead, he graciously invited us inside.

"Please ignore the mess," he said as we entered his living room, which was crammed with charts, planets, and globes.

"Wow," exclaimed Polly. "Are you buildin' a planetarium?"

"Actually, I'm designing a starship."

"What for?"

"Why, for interstellar travel."

I had an eerie feeling about Clark. A premonition of doom. Clark was a braggart. With trouble written all over him. After all, Clark was "Gobbler"!

CHAPTER 17

Gobbler Has a Cow

We were somewhere around Barstow on the edge of the desert when the drugs began to take hold.
—Hunter S. Thompson, *Fear and Loathing in Las Vegas*

"BUMMER RECORD COLLECTION," sighed Polly. "Man."

Polly looked fetching as she browsed on all fours through Clark Gribbet's LPs. Her search only elicited groans.

"Not only does he buy Muzak, he buys it by the yard. He stocked up on cutouts. Mostly Lawrence Welk."

"Can't you find anything hip?" I asked.

"Clark's a momo. He doesn't have dick."

"No Rolling Stones?"

"Naaa. He's into strings."

"He *has* to have Sgt. Pepper's?"

"He has Sgt. Barry Sadler, 'Ballads of the Green Berets.'"

"You're scaring me," I said.

I was coming onto the acid as I scanned Clark's treacly records. We needed some rad tunes to keep our heads in a mellow groove. But he didn't have anything remotely cool—not even The Kingston Trio.

"THERE YOU ARE!" boomed Clark, strolling in with a backslapper grin.

Peter was right behind him, rounding the corner in a zombie trance.

"We were scopin' out your tunes, man," said Polly.

Polly looked gorgeous. We watched her twist a choodie, using only one Zig-Zag.

"Pot is a godsend when you're tripping," said Polly. "It rounds off the edges."

"YOU CAN'T SMOKE THAT IN HERE," croaked Clark. "I WON'T HAVE MY HOUSE SMELLING LIKE AN OPIUM DEN."

Clark looked creepy. His meaty face had an unearthly glow, and his dumpling of a head was starting to melt.

"WOULDN'T YOU PREFER A GLASS OF SHERRY?"

I stared at Clark's blue paisley robe as it took on the mad swirls of Van Gogh's *Starry Night*. Vincent Van Gogh—the patron saint of acid heads.

I watched, bereft of speech, as Clark turned into a giant locust.

"WOULDN'T YOU PREFER A GLASS OF SHERRY?" Clark repeated.

I stared in horror at Clark's giant grasshopper mandibles. Hideous orange goo was oozing from them in sickening spurts.

"Uh, no thanks, man," Polly said.

"WHAT ABOUT A LITTLE MUSIC?" roared the grasshopper.

"I think we should boogie outside and blow this doob," she said.

I grooved on Polly. She had a hip aura. If anyone could get us out of the clutches of this human locust, Polly could.

"I HAVE SOME ROUSING NEW MARCHING MUSIC," boasted Clark. "SHALL I PUT IT ON?"

Clark was absurd. The question was absurd. Once the acid takes over, language becomes absurd, too, if not utterly useless.

"WHAT ABOUT A CARD TRICK? WHO WANTS TO SEE A CARD TRICK?"

Peter was trembling in terror. He gaped at Clark.

"WE COULD ALWAYS PLAY CHARADES," grandstanded our host.

Clark was trying to pal up to us, but his energy was as alien as party favors at a war-crimes trial.

"We should smoke a joint first," advised Polly wisely.

Clark stiffened. There was no way he was going to get in a mellow groove. His entire mission in life was to impress. The first time I saw Clark he was struggling to ride a unicycle on Prospect Street.

"LOOK OUT! GANGWAY!" came his panicked shouts as he sped through the crowd, like a wobbling gyroscope.

The unicycle fad fizzled when he discovered kites. Clark and his festive contraptions were part of the daily landscape. Not an afternoon went by without a sighting of the fat boy in his white knit cap—out showing off his latest toy.

Co-eds watched as Gobbler grunted to the top of Observatory Hill with his cumbersome kite. You could romanticize Clark and compare him to the poet in Baudelaire's "Albatross" whose "giant wings prevent him from walking," but that would be as absurd as Clark and his flight-less kites. And it would be ignoring his noir side—his table manners.

I once had the misfortune of watching Clark eat a 3-D Burger at Howard Johnson's, and the memory stuck to me like the orange Hojo sauce stuck to Clark. If you've dined with college men, you know them for the famine-stricken dung beetles they are. Clark was far, far worse.

His arsenal of gluttony licks put Rotarians to shame.

Polly cleared her throat and consulted her watch.

"Uh... I think we'd better split."

"WHO WANTS TO HEAR ME DO MY BIRD CALLS?"

"Dougie. You were gonna show me around campus," said Polly.

I wanted to reply, but I was engrossed in deciphering the universe. I couldn't utter a sound. Polly squeezed my leg.

"Wouldn't you like to go outside?"

"DO YOU WANT TO SEE MY SLIDES OF THE ICE CAPADES?"

Polly and I stared at each other in mutual horror. We wanted to see some shlub skating around as Mickey Mouse like we wanted to be enslaved by malevolent space aliens.

"WELL, THIS IS JUST RIDICULOUS," Clark said acridly. "IF NO ONE WANTS TO SEE MY MOVIES OR SLIDE SHOWS, THEN, I'M GOING TO BED."

Clark had been dragged out of bed when we arrived, semi-coherent. And now he was saddled with three mental patients.

A door slammed, making us jump.

"Come on, Peter," said Polly, shouldering on her coat.

Peter was blocked in some dark alley of his mind and couldn't find reverse gear.

"OH, MY GOD," he screamed. "I'M MELTING!"

"Ssshh! Don't holler. You'll wake Clark."

"It's just the acid, sweetheart."

"MOMMY," he cried as he flew off the sofa, toppling a lamp.

The lamp landed with a crash on the polished wood floor. Polly righted it and had everything back in place as Clark reappeared.

"WHAT THE HELL WAS THAT NOISE?"

I shrank in my seat as our sleepy host hovered angrily over me.

"Noise?"

"I HEARD A NOISE."

"You did?"

"IF YOU CAN'T BE QUIET, DAMN IT, YOU HAVE TO LEAVE."

"We'll be quiet as church mice."

"ONE MORE PEEP AND YOU HIT THE BRICKS."

Clark went back to bed with his hair sticking up.

Peter had taken off his cuff links and shirt studs, and he was gazing at them as though they were magic gems.

"I'm going to get us something to drink," said Polly. "So, don't move. I mean it, boys. Stay where you are. Run silent, run deep."

I wasn't about to move. I couldn't. I sat on the couch next to Peter and grooved on the acid. I was having the time of my life watching a fountain of color as it seemed to splash from the light of the lamp and then swirl around the room.

"Here, Dougie. Have some Hawaiian Punch," said Polly.

"Wow. Thanks."

"Did you see this?" she asked. Polly took something off the table and showed it to me. It was an engraved sign, the kind you see on office desks. It read: "ONE HUNDRED AND SIXTY IQ, YOU GENIUS."

"Clark's into himself pretty hard-core."

"Show Pete."

We caught Peter Fletcher pouring Hawaiian Punch down the front of his shirt.

"Peter! What the hell are you doing?"

Peter hissed at us. He loitered by the record player in a werewolf crouch.

"Dougie, change the record," said Polly.

"What should I put on?"

"Something mellow. I'll make some blueberry muffins."

I put on the theme from *A Summer Place*—a 1959 soaper with Sandra Dee and Troy Donahue as smitten teens trying to cope with their parents. I had the hots for Sandy. Poor Troy, so compelling as a heartthrob in his heyday, wound up homeless for two years in Central Park.

"Oh, I love this song," called out Polly from the kitchen.

"Me, too."

"What's Spaz doing?"

"Who?"

Polly's tone was imperative. I knew I had to find out what Peter was doing, but the acid had a mind of its own.

I gazed around, in a growing fog. My vaunted primate vision had become kaleidoscopic. Musical notes had form, and they flew from the stereo like autumn leaves.

My voice echoed in an array of distorted permutations.

"Peter?"

Peter was there all the time. He was clomping around the spinning record. Watching him dance was wildly funny at first. Then, his heavy-footed hoofing started making the record skip. This freaked me out. I was afraid he would awaken the giant locust.

"Cut it out, man. You're making the record skip!"

Peter's frenzied dancing skirted the edge of disaster. Clark's furnishings were as fragile as they were expensive. Peter spun past a Tiffany lamp, missing it by a gnat's whisker.

"PETER!"

I implored him to stop. "WATCH OUT, YOU LUMPEN CLOT!"

He wouldn't stop. Or couldn't. He whirled about, an ergot-crazed churl from the Middle Ages.

Now Polly had joined the fray. "KNOCK IT OFF, STUPID!"

Peter didn't get the news flash. There's no BBC World Service in Cloud-cuckoo-land.

"TURN OFF THE FRICKIN' MUSIC, DOUGIE."

I lifted the needle off the record. Peter boogied away like a dancer on Capital Caravan.

I yielded to Polly. She was Rowdy Yates on *Rawhide*.

"I GOT DUCT TAPE. WE'LL BULLDOG THE LITTLE DOGIE. GIT HIM ON THE COUCH. AND HOLD HIS LEGS."

I guided Peter over to the couch and plopped him down. Polly seized a leg and had it between her knees with the dexterity of a wrangler. In a flash, she lashed two throw pillows to Peter's feet with duct tape.

"THAT OUGHTA HOLD THE LITTLE CRITTER."

The pillows worked like a charm. Peter danced away to his heart's content. And without making the record skip.

"Let's watch TV. There's a Rock Hudson movie on."

It was *All That Heaven Allows*, a Douglas Sirk picture. Rock played a hunky gardener with the hots for Jane Wyman. In one scene, Rock's raking leaves at home on top of a hill. Jane pulls into his driveway for the old surprise visit, causing him to *fall off a cliff* as he rushes to greet her.

"That is so Buster Keaton. What a dummkopf."

"Rock Hudson is so dreamy," cooed Polly.

"He can't even futz with leaves, he's such a putz," I said.

"I know," laughed Polly. "But he gives me a total boner."

Douglas Sirk movies are high camp when you're normal. On acid, they're hilarious.

"Did you know that Rock Hudson is a gay guy named 'Roy'?"

"But he's always trying to nail Doris Day."

Doris Day was America's sweetheart. And harder to bag than a Marco Polo sheep.

All That Heaven Allows was a kick. I've never laughed so hard. Then, our local station ran a sign-off number called "Meditation." The music was supposed to be inspirational as you watched some bogus waves crashing on the shore. We sat, transfixed, as the TV drove an existential stake through our hearts.

"Bring me down like the Hindenburg," groaned Polly.

"Let's go to the dorm and get some records."

"We better check on Peter. He's awfully quiet."

The record was over. The stylus made a steady, clicking sound. Polly righted the arm and turned the stereo off. We quietly searched for Peter. He was nowhere to be found.

"Shoot," she sighed. "He's flown the coop."

"Where could he go, with pillows on his feet?"

"Anywhere. Under a bus."

Polly was showing the strain. Her eyes were darty as she scanned the room with clench-jawed apprehension.

I felt a chill of foreboding.

"He's probably gone back to the dorm."

Peter could've stumbled through East Campus and fallen from Prospect down those steep stairs onto M Street.

"Peter's a pathological schmoozer. He'll be in someone's room, dropping names."

"Shouldn't we tell Clark, Dougie?"

I flashed on a giant locust coming after me with orange protoplasmic goo dripping from its mandibles. Space aliens are always drenched in protoplasm. They're clever enough to travel across the galaxy, but too stupid to bring Kleenex.

"We should get the hell out of Dodge." Polly grabbed her purse. She gripped my hand hard and we slipped out the door into the freewheeling streets of night.

Mighty Clouds of Joy

I am happiest when most away
I can bear my soul from its home of clay
On a windy night
When the moon is bright
And the eye can wander through worlds of light—
When I am not and none beside—
Nor earth, nor sea, nor cloudless sky—
But only spirit wandering wide
Through infinite immensity.
—*Emily Brontë, The CompletePoems ,1910*

GEORGETOWN UNIVERSITY WAS AN AMAZING SETTING for a first acid trip. Polly and I were dismayed that someone had removed the pumpkin from Father Carroll's head, but that didn't stop us from having the religious experience of our lives.

"This is so tripped-out Gothic, man."

We puffed to a halt in front of Healy Hall and gazed at everything, in spellbound silence. John Carroll's proposed academy on the Potomac had blossomed into one of America's great universities.

"It's like the grounds of an enchanted castle."

On our way past White-Gravenor, we tried to light cigarettes.

"Forget it. It's too windy."

"Not for my windproof Zippo lighter."

The cigarettes had a comforting effect as we strolled through the chilly air.

"Let's go see the Jesuit graveyard."

The cemetery was a humble affair. Saint Ignatius would've been proud.

"This is the most beautiful place I've ever seen." Polly's voice broke with emotion. We stood before the graves with our hands folded.

"The faith of these men blows me away," I said. "They devoted their lives to educating young men–for centuries. They were the saints of God we used to exalt in our hymns."

"Have you ever known a more sacred place than this?" Polly asked.

"Our little Episcopal church, in Middleburg. Froggie deBordenave was our minister. And my mom and her best friend, Rosalie Grasty, taught Sunday school."

Polly laughed shrilly. She bounded around to stay warm.

"Your minister's name was 'Froggie'?"

"His Christian name was 'Ernest.'"

Polly yelped with delight. She threw her arms in the air and ran around me in circles.

"'Froggie'! That is so *Wind in the Willows*. Did you read...?"

"Of course," I said. "I loved Toad in his motorcar."

"Remember that chapter, 'The Piper at the Gates of Dawn'?"

"When Mole and Rat find God? That is so cool."

"Finding God is what it's all about," Polly said.

Polly was transported. She gave me goosebumps as she steered me into Healy Hall.

"A magic staircase!"

Polly was a sorceress leading me through the enceinte of an enchanted palace. We traipsed down a dark corridor whose walls were sentineled with the murky portraits of notable Jesuits.

"THE SOCIETY OF JESUS. BITCHIN'."

"Sssshhhhhh!"

"Where the hay is Peter?"

"He may be at Britt's."

"What's that?"

"An all-night cafeteria."

"Cool. Will there be lots of freaks?"

"I have some cool friends you haven't met."

"Your friends are straight-arrow Catholic boys."

"They smoke pot."

"In madras jackets? I'd be at another UVA mixer."

"Well, most of the freaks at Britt's are weekend warriors. Trust-fund teenyboppers posturing as hipsters."

"I don't care about hipsters, Dougie. I want to see what the chicks are wearing."

I nodded in agreement. Take a girl to a party, and the first thing she'll do is scope out the competition.

"Let's go see if Pete's in his room."

"Then, we'll go to Britt's," said Polly. "Promise?"

Peter was not in his room in New North, so we made our way across campus to New South.

As we searched the hall, I fixated on a trippy poster some guy had on his door. I was so mesmerized by the poster I must've made a ruckus. Then, to my astonishment, the door issued a huge, hairy dude in sleep-rumpled undies.

"Wow," I muttered, touching his poster.

Satisfied I was a harmless geek trapped in psychedelic flypaper, he closed the door without a word. It was a bizarre moment.

"Holy cow," said Polly. "You're gonna get your ass kicked."

I felt safe tripping on campus. But acid could be hazardous to your health.

"Polly! Look at that wall. Oh, wow!"

Polly studied the cinderblock wall. She didn't see what I saw.

The wall was a swirling tableau vivant of crabs and scorpions. It was a major league hallucination.

"I see scorpions. And crabs. Mostly scorpions."

"Maybe you're a Scorpio?"

"I am a Scorpio," I gasped.

Polly let me groove on the wall. Then, she guided me down the hall.

"Oh, my God," I uttered.

"What's wrong?"

"Look at the beautiful nurses."

There were tunnels under the campus. Malapert students sometimes used them to sneak into the Jesuits' residence and make off with their beer.

"We must've gone through the steam tunnels and come out in the Nursing School," I babbled.

"You're hallucinating. There aren't any nurses."

I saw a roomful of Rhine maidens, all of them dressed in white, and all of them gorgeous.

"I want to see the goddesses."

"You're tripping. It's a bunch of guys in a study lounge."

"You're wrong. I'll prove it."

I led Polly into my erotic Shangri-la only to find a mirage of soph boys burning the midnight oil—or "lucubrating their fill," as Byron would say.

"It's okay, man. It's the acid. First trips are flipped out."

Polly knew her acid. My first trip was the most profoundly enlightening.

"You're not freaking out on me?" asked Polly.

"Jeez. Maybe I shouldn't have done a four-way tab."

"Let's go to Britt's for a hot breakfast."

"Okay. Give me a sec to get my bearings."

Polly cackled with delight as we stumbled back to the safe haven of Healy Hall. Reclining on the regal staircase, we pondered how to resume our search for Peter.

Britt's, the popular cafeteria on Wisconsin Avenue, was a madhouse. Lots of chicks in bells, and cats in headbands. And all of them ripe to rat you out if they pulled so much as a jaywalking charge.

Number one on the list for Hoya Stoolie of the Year was Sted

Egley. Egley would roll over like Fido. He'd drop a dime on his mother just to hear it jangle through the phone.

Britt's. I flashed on all the bogus hipsters I knew. Guys, daring enough to grow sideburns. And chicks, brazen enough to go braless. Guys in army jackets with someone else's name on them—sporting stripes they never earned. And chicks in mod threads they charged to their parents. Kids who booed Hendrix because they wanted to hear The Monkees.

We finally found Peter, no worse for wear, sitting at Britt's in a back booth.

"I copped a wicked good ounce from Sted," he boasted.

"It couldn't possibly be grass," I said.

Peter usually got burned so badly they had to send for his dental records.

"You copped from the Eggplant? Are you nuts?"

"What's wrong with that? Egley's a good kid."

"He's a lush. And a chisel chest. He'll put your business in the street on sandwich boards."

"Don't be such a wimp, my little amigo."

Peter laughed me off. He rolled a jay, and fired it up.

"Hey! No smoking in here," I said. "Britt's has a corporate policy."

"Don't be so paranoid, MacKenzie."

"What about Dean Klumph? He's on the rampage to nail dopers."

"Have a hit, Dougie. It'll mellow you out."

Peter Fletcher was a walking *non sequitur*. And maybe the most affected creature on two feet.

The first time I laid eyes on him, he was stalking out of Healy Hall in a hunter green cape and matching Tyrolean hat.

"Who on earth is that?" I asked my friend, Dan Deming.

We watched Peter as he stage-walked past us in his rakish getup.

"That's Prince Pussytoes. He lives on your hall. He's in Foreign 'Circus'—I mean, Service. They're as rum as they come."

"So you know him?"

"Are you nuts? That crew is blissfully unaware of those of us in

College. So scuttle any plans for making friends."

"That's him. I'm gonna see what he's up to."

"Where were you traipsing off to?" I hailed Peter.

"New South cafeteria," he said curtly, giving me the cold shoulder.

Then, when we were both getting trays in the cafeteria line, I spoke up.

"Hey, I dig your hat."

"Thank you," said Peter crisply.

"Is it a Lester Lanin?" I asked teasingly.

Lester Lanin was a popular bandleader who handed out funny felt fedoras with his signature stitched on them.

"Good heavens, no," said Peter, arching an imperious eyebrow.

"Where'd you get it, then?"

"In Kitzbühel, if you must know."

"I like the brush."

"It's a decorative flourish. Now, if you will kindly move your tray, I shall avail myself of those mashed potatoes."

Peter ignored me along with the desserts. He turned on his heel and headed for the cashier. In the coming weeks, I tried to befriend him a few more times around school, but, each time, he cut me dead. I found out later that he'd taken a lot of ribbing from the other guys, and he was gun-shy when it came to making friends.

"Peter, if you stopped hanging out with three-time losers and social nightmares like Clark Gribbet, you'd catch a lot less grief from the chumps on the hall," I said one day. "And for Christ's sake, drop the phony baloney English accent."

Polly and I relaxed at Britt's. She had the pancakes. I had the three-hour space-out.

Wisconsin Avenue was foggy at 3 a.m. when we walked back outside.

"Where did we park the Plastic Pig?"

"Don't worry. We'll find it."

We found the Vette with the utmost of ease.

"Plastic fantastic," cheered Polly. "Not a scratch."

"I cannot possibly drive."

"Give me the keys."

Polly could've driven Le Mans in the wet. But when she started the car, one of the retractable headlights was stuck. We got out and assessed the situation.

"Push the button while I lift the headlight."

In a flash, both lights were fully operational.

"You know why it wouldn't come up?"

I expected a mechanical explanation, something from Lotus genius, Colin Chapman.

"No," I said. "Why?"

"It was winking," chuckled Polly. "I told ya, he wanted to fuck other cars."

The Dragon's Will

And now we stare astonished at the sea,
and a miraculous strange bird shrieks at us.
—*William Butler Yeats, Her Triumph*

I AWOKE FROM A DREAMLESS SLEEP alone back in the dorm. My brain was a spent flashbulb, with every neuron burnt to a crisp. With some difficulty, I managed to sally forth into the robotic pageant of alarm-clock reality.

Peter and I were so out of the loop, we had trouble finding pot.

"Buy us some decent grass, Douglas. I'm dragooning you into action." Peter squared his shoulders and admired himself in the mirror.

"How do I look?" he asked with a self-satisfied smirk.

"Like a molting Medusa. You had a thousand dollars two weeks ago, and you never paid me back one red cent."

"Well, you deserted me at Clark's. And I broke his Lalique vase. He's bilking me a king's ransom. So there you bloody have it."

Peter sprinkled Royall Lyme cologne and dabbed it about his anatomy.

"Am I your friend, Peter?"

He smiled and drew a damp comb through his flaxen hair.

"Of course you are. You're my roomie."

"Why am I your friend?"

"Because you're so madly charming," he said breezily.

"Then, could I ask you a favor?"

His eyes narrowed with suspicious anticipation.

"Sure," he replied unconvincingly.

"Could I have that last tab of acid?"

"I gave it to Clark," he stated flatly.

"You're kidding?"

"He asked me for it, and I gave it to him."

"You wasted a four-way blue smear on that fascist?"

"Clark Gribbet's not a fascist."

"No. He's a calypso singer. Isn't he on the Student Council?"

"So?"

"And in the Collegiate Club?"

"Clark's as old-school tie as the old Copley Tree. What does that prove?"

"You just gave the A-bomb secret to the Russians."

"I did no such thing. Clark's not a Soviet agent."

"He's Klaus Fuchs with a balalaika."

"Clark will never take the acid. He'll keep it in a drawer to shock people—like Auden did with his revolver at Oxford."

"I don't know. He has a mad-scientist streak, and he's a show-off. I mean, all this business with his flightless kites."

"Douglas," announced Peter in a voice that bespoke the halidom of Hobe Sound, "*I* know Clark. And the Clark I know would *never* experiment with drugs."

"I pray you're right. Woe betide if you're not."

"Clark's an old golfing chum. You can take it to the bank."

"I want to take you first. You owe me four hundred bucks."

Peter puttered with a can of shoe polish and gave his dancing pumps a peremptory buff.

"Fork over a fifty. For auld lang syne," I said.

"You've caught me at an awkward time. My circumstances are temporarily reduced."

"You chintzy chiseler. All week you've been having lobster dinners delivered by the Rive Gauche or somewhere."

"I was on my sickbed, you sadist, and Henri graciously dispatched a little lobster Newburgh to save my life."

"You were playing ping-pong in your pajamas."

"I was at death's icy door, damn it."

"Where are you going?"

"I am getting my great coat from the closet."

"Don't forget your rosary."

Peter shot me a look. He crossed himself, kissed his rosary, then, tucked it in the pocket of his snazzy overcoat.

"I am escorting a Mount Vernon maiden to her debut."

"Lucky you."

"You should see her. She's a Pre-Raphaelite angel. Another evening thronged with sirens. Ah! Poor me."

I pictured him spending an atrocious evening, dancing the bunny hug with mousy girls and suety matrons as an outworn orchestra played "The Old Gray Mare."

Our fights were not a big deal. What worried me was Peter giving Clark the acid.

In five months, Peter's petard would come back to hoist us. Until then, our glowworm of youth was golden, and we shared every scintillating moment in hilariously high style.

We couldn't score any weed for months. Then, we hit it big. A biker I met through Egley could get keys of commercial Mexican for a hundred and fifty bucks. "Steamer" looked like a biker—the black leather edition of John the Baptist—only one who'd spent forty days and forty nights in the buffet line.

"I'm Steamer," puffed the oversized boy. "I'm a hustler."

"DOUG WANTS TO BUY A KILO," boomed Egley.

Patrons at the Peoples Drug lunch counter eyed us with suspicion.

"Why don't you take out an ad in the paper?" I said.

"Sorry, man."

Egley's voice carried like a jungle bird's.

"I'm cool, baby."

Egley was a liability I'd inherited from Peter. The little creep imbedded himself with the dedication of an insect.

I dug Steamer from the jump. Steamer fancied himself a swash-buckler and a renegade, but he still lived in Silver Spring with his mom.

"I'm buying lunch, boys," announced Egley. "Lend me twenty bucks."

Egley smiled. His snaggly teeth were narrow and close. They didn't need an orthodontist as much as a pool cue.

"Hey, *I* made this connection," pressed Egley, making a Whoopee cushion noise with the plastic ketchup bottle. "I should get a finder's fee. If you both chip in a couple of lids, it'll square things with me."

Steamer and I exchanged knowing looks.

"Gotcha," said Egley. "Can I have the rest of your grilled cheese sandwich?"

One of the effects of LSD is an urge to turn others on to the drug. This messianic impulse really hit home with Peter. After he took acid, he couldn't talk about anything else. If you crossed paths with him, you were in for a sermon.

"You really should try acid," I heard Peter telling two startled co-eds standing under the hideous metal globe in Walsh Building.

"No, seriously," he insisted. "It'll change your life."

"NO, SERIOUSLY," he slurred as the pretty pair sloped off in terror. "HEY, I'M TALKIN' TO YOU."

Peter looked embalmed. His eyes were inert and his tongue lolled like a collie's.

We hadn't roomed together long before he started doing downers. The downers were horrid. So was Egley. He seemed to arrive with the reds and, like a migratory bird that suddenly finds things to its year-round fancy, never left.

"WHERE'S FLETCH AT?" Egley would bark while I was sound asleep.

"Get out."

Egley took a quick inventory of our dorm room. His vibe fell between pickpocket and assassin.

"I'm smoking Fletch's stash. He owes me."

"Owes you for what?"

"Writing his English papers."

"You can't even speak English. You end sentences with prepositions."

"You need to think positive."

"No. You need to use adverbs."

My blood pressure soared when I heard Peter's bong burbling away.

"Tell Fletch, if he wants me to use words like 'onomatopoeia,' it's gonna cost extra."

"You're not writing dick, Egley. You're charging Peter fifty a pop for papers you subcontract to Bisley for thirty. And Bisley can't pull anything higher than a 'C.' Peter's paying through the ass for a '2.0.'"

"Who told you I was using Bisley?"

"He's the only school ghostwriter who single-spaces. And make sure you don't hand in Peter's papers for him to Father Ryan, saying his grandmother died."

Egley put down the bamboo bong. "Why not?"

"Because, the third time you did it, Father Ryan asked Peter how many grandmothers he had."

"You're in a rotten mood."

"I WAS ASLEEP, FOR CRYING OUT BLOODY LOUD."

My hands itched for some good weed. If I had a key, I'd have plenty to smoke, and be the life of the party. Making a splash with my peers was more important than something as silly as going to prison. Rashly, I fronted Steamer a hundred and fifty for a kilo of Mexican.

"Steamer's not answering his phone," I told Peter.

Peter's eyes seemed permanently shut. When he moved at all, he took tentative mole steps, using his outstretched arms to maintain his balance. His mouth gaped as his cigarette traced the air in erratic arcs.

"Steamer is doing what, man?"

"Steamer's not answering his phone."

"Then, call the Eggplant. He'll have the inside scoop."

I tried dinging it into Peter to ditch Egley. "Sted's playing you like a fluegelhorn."

"Oh, Douglas."

"He's bad news. When cops see him, they do a U-turn."

"Lemme call Steamer and shake things up," he said.

Peter stood on wobbly legs.

"Are you cool to walk, man?" I asked.

Peter was moving slowly. But he was moving. I waited while he used the pay phone on the landing. To my amazement, he returned with a triumphant smile.

"Steamer's got the stuff! He's meeting us in the Peoples Drugs parking lot in twenty minutes."

There shouldn't have been a lot of traffic on Wisconsin Avenue, but there was. Peter smoked and stared out the window as the Vette crept past the Saville Book Shop. Georgetown had a lot of mom-and-pop charm in those days. The store owners knew you, and you knew them. Folks had more time to chat.

"Drive around the block and check for cops."

"If I do that, I'll just alert the cops."

I dutifully circled the block.

"I need a candy bar," Peter said morosely.

"Couldn't you have gotten a candy bar before we left? Could we score the grass and then get one?" I asked.

Peter angrily scrunched up a chocolate milk carton and began to cry. I tried to comfort him, and he jerked away.

"Don't cry, Peter."

"I'm not crying, Douglas."

"You cry at card tricks. In point of fact, you cried during the movie, *Casablanca*."

"I cry at romance."

"You cried when Major Strasser was shot."

With this, he leapt from the car and sprawled on the pavement. I hopped out to assist him.

"Did I hit some black ice?"

"No. It's that pesky Newtonian gravity."

I practically needed a wheelbarrow to get Peter into the drugstore.

I was afraid we were going to miss Steamer, but the nonchalant fat boy was an hour late. When his patchwork Chevy finally rumbled onto the scene, I was beside myself.

Meeting your connect is the kick. The sight of Steamer's beater with its primer splotches and goitrous hood scoop made my heart flutter. The clomp of his motorcycle boots put me over the moon.

"They didn't have any pot," Steamer joked, with a tug of his beard. "So I got Ripple. Is that okay?"

Steamer was my boy, straight up. Your bitches and ho's may come and go, but your boy will always come through.

"My own boy," I wanted to write Steamer. "Your Slim-Fast soul walks between pasta and poultry."

Steamer dug fried chicken. He never ate anything else. The ounce bags of pot everyone copped from Steamer had the same Colonel Sanders aroma.

I was copping a key, so my spook meter was up. I scanned the busy parking lot for any sign of the heat.

Blue puffs of smoke chugged from the Corvette's side pipes as snowflakes feathered down on the post-Christmas shoppers. I left the engine running so Peter could stay warm, and play the radio. For ten minutes I had warm images of families enjoying Christmas cheer before blazing hearths, and all that good Dylan Thomas stuff.

Then, an icy wind came up, making the snowflakes whirl in swiftly changing eddies. That's when I felt cold. Very cold. End of your dick cold.

Steamer circled the lot like a myopic mallard. In an effort to avoid the law, he exuded more guilt than those busted mutts at the end of Dragnet. Finally, the two-piece Cragar mags ground to a halt.

"Jiminy Christmas. What took ya?"

Steamer gave me a toothy grin. "Are you still interested in getting that pot?"

"No. I'm freezing my ass off for the Green Stamps."

Steamer studied me for a moment.

"Am I late?"

"Only an hour."

Steamer tugged absently on his beard. His car was a sweat lodge of pot smoke and fast food debris. I fidgeted while he idled moronically around the radio dial. When he found The Kingston Trio singing "Tijuana Jail," I prevailed upon him to change it.

"And now, a little smokestack lightning," he joked as he handed me a honking huge brick of dynamite pot.

"Wow. Cool. Thanks, man."

Steamer cocked his head and stroked his beard. "Cool, man," he said easily.

Then, things weren't cool. A metallic rap on the car window made us start like a fright in the night.

"STEP OUT OF THE VEHICLE," ordered an official sounding voice. "YOU'RE BOTH UNDER ARREST."

CHAPTER

20

Murder in my Heart for the Eggplant

*The physician can bury his mistakes, but the architect can
only advise his clients to plant vines.*
—*Frank Lloyd Wright, New York Times Magazine, October, 1953*

FOR A HEART-STOPPING INSTANT Steamer and I were struck dumb with fear and disbelief. The game was up. We were on our way to the slammer. Fuck. I was nailed, with the kilo in my lap. Then, the car door opened, and I stared at the arresting officer. Instead of an undercover narc or uniformed bull, there stood Egley.

"That's real funny, asshole."

Egley doubled over with laughter.

"That is an anemic attempt at humor," groused Steamer.

"You should see your faces. I'll bet you pissed your pants."

Egley smiled vilely. "Okay, man. Where's my shake?" With this, he wedged himself into the car. I was pressed in between him and Steamer. Egley helped himself to Steamer's menthols.

Egley made Judas a stock character. You could picture him garnering "Employee of the Month" during the reign of terror.

"Got a light?" he demanded. When Egley pushed in the car lighter, Steamer switched off the ignition.

"You're the missing link between ape and rodent, Egley," said Steamer.

"Got a match? Who's got a match? I need a light."

"Get out," growled Steamer.

"Who rattled your cage? I just need a match."

When fear stripped Egley to bare metal, what remained was pure con. "Hey, man. You're talkin' to the Eggplant. Who loves ya, baby?"

"Get out," repeated Steamer.

"You're a couple of killjoys. What did I do?"

Steamer was quietly furious. "Get out of my car."

It was high tide at Testosterone Beach. Egley and Steamer sprang from the car. It didn't take a lip reader to know what was being said out in the parking lot. Egley was in Steamer's face, shouting obscenities. He had on a sky-blue double-breasted mod coat with outsized lapels.

Egley instigated the fight by shoving Steamer. The big boy fell hard in the snow. When he got back up, Egley came at him again. Sted was the bearbaiter. Too quick for Steamer, he nipped in with vicious slaps and shoves.

Usually at the first hint of trouble, I head for the hills. But I was not about to abandon my superfly score of primo smoke.

"Come on, fatso," taunted Egley. "Take your best shot."

Steamer was winded. Blowing smoke in the wintry air, he didn't have a best shot. I winced as Egley was on him again, landing unanswered blows. Then, the strangest thing happened.

Steamer let loose a George Foreman right hand that caught Egley flush on the left eyebrow. It was a monster wallop on a time delay, and it spun Sted around like a spin rack. I erupted with joy and pounded the car seat.

"Did you see that?" cried Sted. "The psycho hit me." Blood spurted from Egley's head as he sat sprawled in the snow.

"ASSAULT AND BATTERY," cried Egley. "YOU SAW IT, FOLKS."

"Why'd you have to hit him so hard?" demanded Peter.

"He was asking for it," panted Steamer.

"Douglas, help me get him in the car."

"He's not getting in my car."

"I need a doctor," screamed Egley theatrically. "I'm bleeding."

"Let's get him to the hospital. He's gonna need stitches."

"My coat," wailed Egley. "My beautiful coat."

I was loath to take Egley to the hospital. I wanted to take him to the police station and have the K-9s do a full cavity search. There was nothing wrong with Egley that a hyperthyroid German shepherd couldn't fix.

"Okay," I said. "But don't get any blood in my car."

Steamer flipped me my stash. I stuffed it under the Corvette seat. Peter and Sted piled in the car as I gingerly drove out of the parking lot.

"Step on it," barked Egley. "You drive like a pussy."

The trek to Georgetown Hospital really got my heart pumping. It was snowing like a bitch, and I couldn't see. I had to drive at a snail's pace to keep the Vette from sliding off the road. Then, I got the fright of my life. A squad car was suddenly on my ass, with the cherries going and the siren keening. I pulled over with my heart in my mouth, and the black-and-white zoomed by. The rollers were after someone else. Whew.

"You should see your face." Egley's laugh was dark and sadistic. "Get popped with a key, you'll do a year in the can."

"Shut up, Egley."

The words were scarcely out of my mouth when I tried to brake for a stop sign and slid straight through an intersection. Thankfully, no cars were coming. I breathed a sigh of relief, which Peter punctuated by lighting a joint.

"WHAT ARE YOU DOING, ASSHOLE?" I cried.

In his Isadora Duncan muffler, Peter looked like The Little Prince.

"God. You are so paranoid," he said.

Why Peter tolerated Sted Egley was a mystery. While Peter was highly sought after as a bridge partner, when Egley dropped by, they played "War." It was the only game Sted knew.

Egley needed fifteen stitches. The procedure cost fifteen bucks. Sted couldn't come up with a dime, so I ponied up ten and Peter threw in five.

Egley told the attending physician he "fell in the shower."

I never expected to see my ten bucks and didn't. But later,

whenever Egley put the squeeze on me, I'd just ask him for my money.

"I'm a little short this week," he'd whine. "I'm getting a check tomorrow" was a routine reply.

The kilo was gone in three days. You don't push weed; it sells itself.

But dealing is a bore—especially in college. College kids are flaky about finance. They want their dope fronted, and then never pay you. Or they piss and moan about the seeds, stems, price, weight, or whatever. And they have to hang out with you for hours every time they cop. Then they eat your last yogurt, and leave pubic hairs in the bathtub.

"I'm too wasted to split, man. I may have to crash here."

"I'd rather you didn't."

"Freaks are all brothers, man. Everyone shares."

Maybe the hippie ethos worked in Taos. But in the utopias I saw, the rich hippies wound up at the bottom of the pyramid. And when they wised up and cut off the carte blanche, their houseguests split for greener pastures. Mooches were on the move in the Silver Sixties. Their mass migrations rivaled those of the Mayans.

My big score proved a poison chalice. From the day I copped, Egley plagued me like a bubonic rat. Everywhere I turned, Sted was there with his awful teeth, putting the bite on me. Every street corner was impregnated with the image of Egley in his blue coat. It got so bad, I could spot blue coats at a thousand yards.

Happily, I had a new girlfriend and wasn't around much.

———⊷—⊶———

My new mango lassie was named Mandy. Mandy Pringle. Mandy was quite a departure after Edie and Polly. Mandy was a doll. She was so nice, she could've played Snow White. Tadger and I had come a long way from our pavement princess in Place Pigalle.

Mandy fell for me first. When we started sleeping together, I forthrightly announced I was in love with Polly Hay. This set the hook in Mandy though I hadn't intended it to.

Mandy and I clicked at a dance at the Springs Club in Warrenton, Virginia, in 1967. It was a warm night during the Summer of Love. The band was the Jaguars, a local greasy kid-stuff cover group whose members all sported red blazers.

Once you got by the blazers and Wild Root Cream oil, the Jaguars were a fave rave. If we couldn't have the Yardbirds, we'd settle for our yeomanly, near-beer knockoffs.

Anything beat your parents' music. They dug orchestras that couldn't rock out if their lives depended on it. Requesting hip tunes from these blue-rinse heads didn't help. Swing-era cats are not gonna know "Louie Louie."

I was dancing with Mandy at Moira Archbold's in Georgetown, later that autumn, when she prompted me to have the band play "something cool."

"Oh, right. You want me to ask Guy Lombardo to play 'Hot Nuts'?"

I was totally baked, and figured, why not, right? So I sidled up to the bandleader and asked for "something cool."

"Something cool?" he asked, staring glassily.

"You know. Something fast. Like the Telstars."

I was asking a rabbi to raid Entebbe. The bandleader looked harrowed.

"Ze Telstars?" he croaked. "You mean... *Schputniks?*"

"Rock and roll. Like on *American Bandstand.*"

A light went on. He smiled and laughed with relief. "Ah, sure, young man. *American Bandstand.*"

I returned to Mandy, thinking I'd connected. The orchestra rewarded my efforts with a lamester version of "Palisades Park." Oh, well. It was better than "Tiny Bubbles."

I can't remember what was playing the first time I kissed Mandy Pringle. What a kiss! We kissed with youthful passion as my hands cupped her ass. She had the best ass, Mandy did, wow! It was heart shaped, like a valentine from God.

"The last time I saw you, you chased me with a water pistol."

"*Plus ça change,*" I laughed.

Mandy laughed. She had intelligent blue eyes and a little Betty Boop mouth. Her hair was dark brown and cropped short. When her hair was long, she looked like Edie Sedgwick in those photo-booth snaps.

"I never see you at parties, Doug. Are you still living at 'Journey's End'?"

"Journey's End" was my childhood home in Middleburg. Pamela and Averell Harriman bought "Journey's End" from us in 1977, and renamed it "Willow Oaks."

In C. David Heymann's book, *The Georgetown Ladies' Social Club...*, Heymann reveals that Pamela Harriman "was kind to three women. One was Millicent West." My mom, Millicent, liked to tell how Pam made her laugh.

"I phoned Pamela after she'd been named Ambassador to France," she said:

"'Congratulations, Pamela,' I gushed. 'You've covered yourself in glory.'

'Millicent, dear girl,' riposted the newly-minted diplomat, with mock solemnity. 'The only glory I seek is in my hydrangeas.'"

"I spent the last two summers in France," I told Mandy.

"Cool. Then, you haven't seen my new car; it's a '62 TR-4. It's burgundy, with a black top."

"Get outta here. You have a TR-4? I love those."

Mandy and I went out into the parking lot at the Springs Club.

"It's tiny," I marveled.

We climbed into the Triumph. I nestled into the driver's seat and gripped the wheel.

"I love the smell of sun-baked leather. It's really nice. Did you see my Vette?"

"Did you get that for graduation?"

"I got it because I ran away from school. Dad bribed me with the car to go back."

"You're bad."

"I know. I want to be like Charlie Parker."

"A musician?"

"No. Chronically disheveled."

"Where did you go when you ran away?"

"Bob Kreuzberg and I were going to Myrtle Beach to fish chicks."

"How'd you do?"

"We got pulled in for vagrancy."

"Being a bum is hard work. I'm going to Mary Baldwin College in the fall, and I'm majoring in sociology."

"How come?"

"I want to help people."

"I wish you'd help me."

"Help you do what?"

"Unhook this."

"It unhooks in the front. Here."

Mandy was no flower child, but she had big plans for saving the human race. As a social worker, she'd spend many a steamy afternoon driving down dirt roads to assist the aged, aid the infirm, and help the needy.

"What are you majoring in at Georgetown?"

"Well, I was majoring in animal husbandry, until they caught me."

"Seriously?"

"French."

"That sounds challenging. Are you thinking of becoming a diplomat?"

"I'm thinking of committing acts of gross debauchery."

Mandy pondered this as I kissed her breasts.

"You don't consider debauchery a human failing?"

"The only human failing is to believe the world is real."

"That's very Buddhist. Have you read *Siddharta*?"

"Only the comic book."

"If you're interested in Buddha, you should read it."

"I don't care about Buddha."

"You're not seeking enlightenment?"

"Not that I know of."

"Well, what are you looking for?"

"Someone sexy who can cook dinner."

"A gourmet hooker?"

"Now we're talking."

"That's very Buddhist. Siddharta claimed he learned more from prostitutes than he did from the holy men."

I had little Mandy on the boil. She seemed ready to make love.

"Scootch over, doll baby."

"There's nowhere to scootch."

"We could get in my Corvette. It's bigger."

"It's late. The parking lot's just about empty."

"What should we do?" I asked.

"Why don't you ask me out on a real date?"

"Dating is so artificial. And pressure packed."

"Pressure packed? I hope putting your hand in my pants didn't give you an ulcer."

"What about a movie?"

"You just want to take me to the drive-in."

"What's wrong with that?"

"They have horrible movies."

"I know. But who cares?"

"I care," said Mandy firmly. "Zip me up."

"I know a really good movie."

"What is it?"

"It's a French movie called *A Man and a Woman*."

"Where's it playing?"

"At the Janus, on Connecticut Avenue. How does Saturday night sound?"

"Fine."

"I'll pick you up at six."

That was how I hooked up with Mandy. After that, I saw her whenever I could, that summer, and for the next ten years.

Mandy was such a dream goddess. She looked more homecoming queen than valedictorian.

"Saturday night, at six. Great. Oh, and Doug...?"

"Yeah?"

"You should read *The Razor's Edge*."

"Who's it by?"

"Somerset Maugham. It'll make you want to go to India."

"Okay, sweetheart. Night, night."

India? I wanted to go to Daytona and watch Dan Gurney drive his 289 Cobra on the high banking. But India?

As farfetched as it seemed, Mandy would get her wish, and I'd be the one to fulfill it for her.

In eight years, we'd be driving the Grand Trunk Road through the Hindu Kush and the thirty-one-mile-long Khyber Pass to monsoon-flooded Lahore and on to Amritsar—our first Indian city. What a day that was! And what a sense of triumph we shared as we sat in the sun outside Indian Customs with a pandemonium of parrots in the trees above. We had the subcontinent of Mother India before us. Mandy and me. And it all started with a kiss.

CHAPTER 21

Sleeping Together

Girls, girls, girls were made to love.
—*Phil Everly, The Everly Brothers, "Girls Girls Girls"*

MY FIRST DATE WITH MANDY was groovy. Mandy wasn't fazed when we were going full cry to D.C. in the Pig. We blistered the road outside her house and rocketed away like Don "Big Daddy" Garlits smokin' another railie in his Swamp Rat.

"WHAT'LL THIS THING DO?"

"VAL PUSTER AND I HAD IT UP TO ONE THIRTY-SIX COMING BACK FROM VIRGINIA BEACH."

"WHAT WERE YOU DOING IN VIRGINIA BEACH?"

"Raisin' hell," I said, as we motored onto Route 66. "Getting hassled by the man. The cops impounded my car. We came out of Sambo's, and it took us two hours to figure out it was towed."

"Were you down there for Spring Break?"

"We were celebrating RMA graduation."

"Was it 'Surf City'? 'Two girls for every boy'?"

"It was Scurf city. Ten sutures for every lush. And two more speeding tickets for me. A K-9 cop gave me one for going five miles an hour over the limit. Have you ever been down there?"

"Never," said Mandy over the burble of side pipes. "We stay in Nag's Head. It's beautiful."

[173]

"Do you want to get a bottle of cough syrup before the movie and get wrecked? I have a buddy named Henry in Alexandria. Henry said, if you drink a whole bottle of cough syrup, you'll hear music."

Mandy laughed. "Kicks just keep getting harder to find."

"You don't know anyone who has any grass?"

"At Fauquier High in Warrenton, Virginia? Not really."

"You like to smoke grass, don't you?" I asked.

"Grass makes me psychiatric," she said. "But I don't mind if you smoke it."

"Well, what do you like to do?"

Mandy flicked her Tareyton out the window and sidled her curvy bottom over next to me. She made a throaty purring noise when she breathed in my ear and nibbled my earlobe.

"Jeepers creepers," I gasped.

"I like to fool around," she said in a husky whisper.

My heart was really going. Her wet mouth gave me goose bumps. It didn't take Dinah Shore to know she wanted to see the USA in my Chevrolet. I saw a parking space.

"What are you doing?" she asked.

"I'm gonna run into Peoples Drug and get some Robitussin."

"Where are we?"

"Dupont Circle."

"You know your way around."

"My dad's from Chevy Chase."

"Leave the engine running so I can listen to the radio."

I left Mandy with John Coltrane playing "My Favorite Things" on soprano sax, an instrument Sidney Bechet introduced to jazz.

"Sit tight, sweetheart. I'll be back in a flash."

Or so I thought. Then it was disorder at the border with some thrombotic midget from Korea who didn't speak English making life a living hell at the cash register.

It never fails. You can go through a checkout in a breeze nine out of ten times. But when you have the fuck of your life waiting in the car, you get stuck behind a reject from Pakistan who has twelve forms of ID, and none of them valid. So the Asian overachiever, who's more anal than Captain Ahab, makes poor Ahmed call Karachi so he can get his fucking check cleared for a goddamned dollar twenty-nine box of Q-Tips–JESUS FREAKING CHRIST!

"Sorry I took so long."

"That's okay."

"Here's your Robo."

"Bottoms up."

"Cheers."

A *Man and a Woman* was one of the great date movies. In it, sexy-voiced Jean-Louis Trintignant plays a race driving widower with a young son. So, guess whom he meets when he's dropping off his kid at school? The recently widowed and eminently munchable Anouk Aimée, that's who. Anouk has a kid, too, so they hit it off. Anouk spends the rest of the movie flipping her hair. Jean-Louis drives all over France with a worried look on his face while Francis Lai's captivating score plays in the background.

"Can you hear any music yet?" I asked Mandy.

"No. But I feel like I have a hat on."

The cough syrup was a bust.

On our next date Mandy and I double-dated with Kitty Symington and my old friend Carter, who was a freshman at UVA. Carter was a tall Virginian with astonishing blue eyes and an Irish wit. Kitty was a pretty girl from Rochester, New York.

Carter drove his gray MGB-GT on The Plains Road like Brian Redman in the Targa Florio. At UVA, he terrorized Fraternity Row in his Milano Maroon 1966 Corvette Coupe.

"I'd love to double-date. But you'll have to drive. Those surly bastards down in Richmond yanked my operator's permit," I said.

"How déclassé," Carter laughed.

"I can't think of anything I did wrong. It's all so Franz Kafka," I said.

"I heard you tried to make a Corvair fly."

"The flight wasn't so bad. But the landing was a bit dodgy."

"Okay, Douglas. I'll come by your dorm when I get to D.C.

"I have Air Force ROTC, which I'm thinking about ditching because they keep giving me grief about my hair."

On our way to Staunton to pick up Mandy, Carter and I embarked on a social whirl that began at The Tombs and wound up at the Washington Hilton on 16th Street. Through what logical progression we ended up at this destination, I couldn't venture to say.

It was from here that our best-laid plans for best getting laid went awry. A "nightcap" became "one for the road," and at 2 a.m. we were still pounding potables with some Holyoke chicks who put the stuff away like they had wooden legs.

Carter was all smiles and tasseled loafers as we called it an evening and made our way down in the elevator. We walked past Trader Vic's, President Nixon's favorite restaurant.

"Hey, Douglas, guess what? I just dropped acid."

"You're fucking with me, right?"

Carter issued a mad laugh and clapped me on the back. "They said it was acid. I guess we'll find out."

My heart sank. "May I remind you we have a date tomorrow—to meet Mandy and Kitty—at Mary Baldwin. In Staunton. How are you gonna drive?"

Carter laughed. He took a key on a leather fob and tossed it to me, underhand.

"*You're* gonna drive," he said curtly.

"Fuck. I don't have my license."

"That's never stopped you in the past."

"Oh, terrific," I said dismally. "It's a four-hour drive."

I wheeled the MG onto K Street and headed for Georgetown. My hopes that Carter wouldn't be tripping were quashed at the Little Tavern on Wisconsin. It was here my elongated amigo came unglued. I was chomping down a large Little Tavern burger with extra onions when Carter drew my attention to the front page of the *Washington Post*.

"Look at this," he exclaimed excitedly.

I wiped ketchup from my mouth and took a sip of black coffee.

What Carter wanted me to see were some photos of some dour-looking men and their latest diplomatic postings. Under the photo of a particularly geeky-looking fellow was the caption: "Turkey."

Carter burst out laughing. I was so punchy, it cracked me up, too.

"TURKEY!" he shrieked, in stitches.

At this point, I knew the acid was kicking in.

"Now, you boys settle down," growled the surly ex-Marine behind the counter as he cooked ground beef patties on the hissingly hot grill.

Our hijinks were not winning the hearts and minds of our fellow Little Tavern patrons. Granted, normal consciousness may be one drop in an ocean of intelligence. Yet it's normal consciousness that comes in handy for routine stuff like keeping saber-toothed tigers off your ass.

"Let's hit the trail. What an old blowfish," clucked Carter as I paid our check and we struck off into the night.

"Slime gods fear no man," I said.

Carter's spirits soared at the mention of the slime gods.

Not all acid helps you find God. Some of it only makes you laugh. And that's what Carter and I took one dog-lazy night in Middleburg with the cicadas whirring in the lilac and the hoot owls hooting from the deep woods along Goose Creek.

"Do you hear water?" I asked as we drove through the tiny hamlet of Aldie.

"It could be water from the millrace. Let's take a look."

Carter and I became Frank and Joe Hardy as we left John Mosby Highway for an unlit dirt road. The mystery was solved when we came upon a lovely little waterfall that neither of us knew existed.

"It's a secret waterfall."

We gazed at the waterfall for a moment before splashing into the shallow stream to get under it. The rush of water felt amazing as we pressed ourselves into the mouth of the torrent. At the very heart of the cataract, we communed with the life-giving water nymphs and wantoned in their slippery embrace.

When our mystical experience subsided, I noticed we were covered in aquatic plant life from head to toe.

"Carter, look. We're green."

"Wow."

"We're covered with algae. We better get back to the car."

"We're Slime Gods," avowed Carter, throwing out his arms, "and Slime Gods fear no man."

I scampered through the woods, with Carter in close pursuit. You could smell the honeysuckle and hear tree frogs as we trotted down the dirt road, with a newly risen full moon looming behind us. It was a night of rare calm as we loped along, covered in green, with Carter giggling to himself behind me.

Then, what sounded like a pistol shot shattered the night air and scared the bejesus out of us. It was a car backfiring and approaching us from behind.

This threw us into a panic, but before we could react, we found ourselves in the blinding glare of headlights.

"Shit," cried Carter. "Now we're fucked."

"Oh, crumbs."

"What should we do?"

"Haul ass. RUN!"

We made a run for it. But the car switched off its lights and matched our speed as we bounded along. This made things even creepier, to say the least.

"Jesus. What are they doing?"

"They're hunting us. Like animals."

The car was a beat-up old Packard that belonged in a demolition derby.

"It's a bailing wire special."

"Who's driving?"

"I can't tell."

The phantom jalopy eerily kept its distance. At last its air of menace got the best of Carter. He hitched up suddenly, skirting the ditch as he scoped out the vehicle's occupants. What he saw filled him with terror.

"FEET DON'T FAIL ME NOW. RUN FOR YOUR LIFE!" he cried.

CHAPTER 22

Icarus Laments

The happy whore fuckers
Are satisfied and fit;
While my poor arms are trashed
From humping only clouds.

——*Charles Baudelaire, "Les Plaintes d'un Icare," (translation by D. MacKenzie)*

YOU'VE NEVER BEEN CHASED until you've been chased by mysterious strangers in the middle of the night while tripping on LSD and covered with green slime.

"This way!" cried Carter. He ducked into the dark trees beside the road. I plunged into the spot where he disappeared and nearly tripped over his crouching figure.

"Look out! What're you doing?"

Carter collapsed to the ground, laughing, as we hid in the trees, watching the old Packard disappear in a cloud of dust.

"I was hoping they'd take a victory lap."

"Man, we fruck them out. They probably thought we were *Creature From the Black Lagoon.*"

And so the legend of the Slime Gods was born.

Some of our acid trips were bummers. The night Carter dropped at the Hilton without confiding in me proved disastrous.

I drove Carter quickly back to campus and the safety of Healy Hall.

"You stay here. Don't move. I'll be right back."

I left my wigged-out amigo in a safe place and hotfooted it over to New North. I had hoped we would be able to stay in my room until dawn. Then we could book down to Mary Baldwin College in Staunton and pick up the chicks.

"Peter," I said, with an urgent knock. "Open up. It's me."

I could hear music, but whoever was in the room wouldn't open the door.

"The door's locked, Carter. We're gonna have to hit the road."

Carter was frozen in the same spot where I'd left him. He'd taken my warning not to move to heart, and he stood, stock still, with an astonished look on his face.

"Ease up there, chief. I didn't tell you to be Lot's wife."

Silence.

"Dude. It's okay to move. Shake a leg, hoss. Time's a wastin'. "

Carter was Gonesville.

"If we play our cards right, we can nail a pair of red-hot muffies."

"WHAT?" he squealed.

"I'm not asking you to be Cary Grant. Just be cool. Let me do the talking, and try not to make eye contact."

Carter gaped at me.

"I know," I said. "We could go down to the gym and shoot some hoops."

"WHAT?"

McDonough Gym was still big enough for the basketball team in 1968. Back then, the Hoyas were still a bunch of short white guys shooting foul shots underhand.

"AND NOW PLAYING FOR THE PRINCETON TIGERS... FROM CRYSTAL CITY, MISSOURI... A SIX-FIVE SENIOR AND THREE-TIME ALL-AMERICAN... THE CENTER... NUMBER 42... *BILL... BRADLEY*!"

My voice echoed in the empty gym. Carter sat perched on the sidelines as I drained a succession of jump shots.

I waved for Carter to join me at the foul line, but he wouldn't move. Wouldn't or couldn't, I figured he'd be normal by the next day.

"Come on, Gilligan. We're gonna go meet Mary Ann and Ginger."

If you can babysit a houseplant, you can care for an acid victim.

"Put your coat on. We're going to Warrenton," I said.

Imagine marching a zonked-out maniac through a morning of workaday reality. Imagine ordering breakfast at the Howard Johnson's in Warrenton in the company of a rabbit-eyed lunatic. And imagine that it actually happened, and that we managed to pull it off without a hitch. Well, almost.

"Good morning, Dottie," I said to the waitress. "My friend and I would like two fried eggs, sunny-side up, and...."

"WHAT'S HAPPENING?" screamed Carter startling every customer half out of their wits.

"And a newspaper," I added, not missing a beat. "So we can find out what's happening."

Dottie's not buying it. She was a flinty-eyed rank-and-filer whose job description did not include bringing two drug-addled weirdos a newspaper.

"Oh, and some toast and er... uh... some bacon, too, please."

Dottie looked old as a moon rock, though she was probably only on the squinty side of sixty.

"How'd y'all like gat bacon cooked?"

Dottie was a local. Her cotton candy perm proved it. It was great being back in Warrenton where I could marvel at hairstyles that have been extinct longer than the giant penguin.

Dottie was a compact woman with the perpetually raised penciled-in eyebrows of the Southern belle. She hunched over like a crow huddling against the cold on a snowy morning.

"How would you like your bacon cooked?" I said.

It's not a trick question, but Carter "snodgrasses" it, anyway. "My *what*?" he muttered.

"Your bacon, man. How would you like it prepared?"

Carter just stared. I couldn't tell if he was gonna answer or flame out.

"He's been cramming for exams," I offered cheerfully. "And he'd like his bacon not too crispy, please."

Dottie paused with her pencil.

"Not too crispy," she droned in a backwoods twang.

Carter and I got the red carpet at Howard Johnson's and feasted like stevedores. I hoped a hot meal would sober him up, but no dice. Two cups of java, and he was still crazier than a certain type of rat.

Then, when I was sure we'd alienated Dottie, she brought us *The Fauquier Democrat*. At 6 a.m., with hours to kill, I read about prize Herefords, a record pumpkin, and a local boy killed in Vietnam.

Then it was time to go. With full tummies, we headed south on Route 29 towards Charlottesville.

I knew I was on the right road when I got near Opal and saw the gun shop bear.

"There's Clark Brothers, Carter. Do you think it's too early for target practice?"

Carter's MGB-GT was a sweet-handling delight. Its tiny four-banger purred along as we passed trucks on a long, sweeping turn entering Albemarle County.

"So many beautiful farms," I said.

The MG had a delicious note. I could feel it resonate through my fingertips.

"That's a sweet sound for a stock exhaust."

The 1800-cc engine was on full song. We carved through traffic in a flash of wire wheels. Morris Garage built nearly four hundred thousand MGBs. There was even an MGC-GT, but its bigger six-cylinder compromised the handling.

"I feel like Jim Clark winning the Indy 500. What a cool car!"

Carter still didn't respond.

"Here we are. Back at your dorm at good old UVA. Put on some clean threads. Then, we can bounce."

Getting Carter dressed took forever.

At long last, we were out the door and headed for Mary Baldwin College.

"Staunton! Birthplace of Woody Wilson!"

I parked on a side street where Carter and I could have a final pep talk.

Carter just gaped and grunted.

"Let's book. It's time to meet the chicks."

Once on campus, we stopped to catch our breath. I maintained my happy-go-lucky Andy Hardy pose as whip-smart girls went by, books in arm, on their way from class.

"Come on, Boris. Time for meeting Moose and Squirrel."

A smoking hot blonde chick smiled at us, and Carter stopped to groove in her wake.

"Keep moving, man. It's not chic to drool."

I clapped an arm around stilt boy and squeezed.

"We're meeting the girls in some reception deal. But I have no idea where it is. Maybe we should ask."

I heard folk music, and folk music spelled chicks. "Let's go in. They're playing Joni Mitchell." We shuffled through an elegant foyer and ran smack into our dates. Kitty gave me the leaning chick hug with no boob contact. She was radiant in a navy jumper and all smiles when she scoped Carter.

"Hello, Carter," she cooed in a lovesick lilt.

"Hi," managed her swain in a tremulous squeak.

"Hi, Dougie."

"Hi, Mandy."

"Did you have trouble finding us?"

"A little. Sorry we're late."

Mandy was impeccably tailored in a grey pinstriped shirtdress. Her breasts felt soft as she gave me a warm hug.

"It's so good to see you. What a cool dress."

"It's so grey. I feel like a Soviet war monument."

"I was about to say, you can stand atop the tractor factory in Smolensk."

Mandy laughed politely. "I brought you a book. It's a new collection of John Keats' letters."

"Keats was the only poet who knew less about women than Shelley."

"Do you still have your pet 'possums? I remember coming to see you at 'Journey's End' with Mama. You were sick in bed. With your 'possums peering out from under the covers."

"Everyone said they'd bite me. But they never did."

"You really like my dress? It's from Thalimer's."

Our little parlor visit was on a happy note until Kitty crossed the room, looking very grim.

"What's wrong with Carter?" she asked, near tears.

"What's he doing?"

"Staring at the wallpaper. He won't speak to me."

Carter stood alone by the window, with his arms limply at his side. He was a sad Harlequin.

"What is wrong with him, Douglas?"

Kitty wiped her nose with her handkerchief and gave me a baleful stare. We were stuck in that scene from *Planet of the Apes* where Charlton Heston howled with outrage, "YOU CUT UP HIS BRAIN, YOU BLOODY BABOON!"

Mandy sat back on the leather couch. When she crossed her legs, my heart skipped a beat. I wanted to take her to the nearest motel, and make a religion out of her scrumptie.

"Carter's beat. He's been working like a dog," I explained,

Kitty broke down in tears. Mandy tried to console her, but she couldn't stop crying.

"We'd better go," announced Mandy resolutely "What are you doing *next* weekend?"

"Seeing you, I hope."

"Call me, Dougie."

Carter and I left Mary Baldwin and took the long drive back to D.C.

"Where are we going?"

"Chain Bridge. Less traffic."

"Wow," said Carter, turning up the radio. "Listen to this."

I pulled up in front of Healy Hall as John Lennon sang "Across the Universe."

"We have to hear this," insisted Carter.

I nodded. When the music was over, we shook hands goodbye, and Carter folded his long frame into the little car. I waited as he fussed with his driving gloves and adjusted the bucket seat.

"You look like Dan Gurney. Ready to do battle."

Carter's bright blue eyes were shot through with red. He flashed a big smile as he popped the clutch in a chirp of tires, and gave a farewell wave as he headed back to Virginia.

I waved back as the MGB-GT tore across "The Yard" before exiting campus onto O Street. Then, I darted back into my dorm and gave old Mandy a call.

Watching the Defectives

This is the space age. Time to look beyond this run down radioactive cop rotten planet.
—William S. Burroughs, in Literary Outlaw, by Ted Morgan

I LOVE HISTORY. If I have a chance to tour a battlefield, I take it. When Mandy Pringle and I were in Belgium in 1971, we spent an afternoon at Waterloo. It was a brilliant summer day, so we had ample time to tramp the field of rye and clover where so many men and horses came to grief.

"Fifteen thousand English soldiers died here on a Sunday afternoon. This is where they stopped Napoleon."

Mandy shielded her eyes from the sun and gazed solemnly across the placid plain of wavy, green grass.

"They weren't all English," I said. "Napoleon was impressed by the courage and discipline of the Scots Greys. Wellington's Highlanders were the mortar in the British squares."

"I know. They took the full brunt of the Imperial Guard."

"Byron was here in 1816—a year after the battle. Small boys were hawking buttons as souvenirs. He liked the plain of Waterloo, but not as much as Troy and Marathon."

"So when you think of Waterloo, you think of Byron?" she asked.

"Sure. The Waterloo stanzas of Childe Harold bring the battle to life. 'There was a sound of revelry by night.' Oh, it's great stuff! 'How in the noon of night that pibroch thrills...'"

"What's a *pibroch*?"

"A set of variations for the Highland bagpipes."

"You're taken with Byron because he was half Scottish?"

"And because he was funny. Lord Byron was the Monty Python of Regency England."

"The Brits couldn't whip Napoleon alone. They needed the Prussians to finish off La Grande Armée. Oh, well."

Mandy was keen on wax museums. I found them dreary. I grudgingly went to Madame Tussaud's because "a man has to keep his woman happy." That's why we say stuff like: "Louisa May Alcott? Why, I adore Louisa May Alcott."

"You do?"

"Of course. If you want to see *Little Women*, we'll see *Little Women*."

"You don't mind?"

"Naaa. I can watch the Indy 500, and the shaved French supermodels on the Playboy Channel, some other time."

"Are you sure?"

"I don't want to have these marbled New York strips and cold Tuborgs if it means missing Susan Sarandon. I hear her feminist monologues are fantastic."

"Can we bring 'Woofy'?"

"No problem. We can easily fit a Great Pyrenees in my new 360 Modena. He's been in the pond all day? Well, a little water never hurt anything."

"Can we bring my ex-boyfriend?"

"The more the merrier."

"He's been up for a week, tweaking off crystal."

"Great. I enjoy methamphetamine users. They're so outgoing. Maybe he could bring a friend."

———◆———

One of the perks of courting Mandy was the relief it gave me in avoiding Egley. But it was spring semester, time to hit the books, and I was back in the *saxa* again.

"Sted was looking for you," said Peter.

"Tell him I joined the foreign legion."

"Fine," said Peter, "I'll dodge him as well."

"Why the change of heart?"

"Second semester sweep. It's when we traditionally ditch the bungwads and yohobs we befriended first semester. So, you're lamming it at Tehaan's?" he asked.

"You better believe it, Buster Brown," I laughed.

Tehaan's, at 36th and Prospect, was a Hoya favorite for eons. In 1919, it was still a general store with a soda fountain. By 1967, the general store had become a cozy diner staffed by conversable soul sisters in spiffy white uniforms.

Tehaan's was where I'd breakfast on French toast, bacon and big, brown farm-fresh eggs. My proprietary booth was in the back, facing the door *à la* Wild Bill Hickok. It was the perfect hideout. I'd hang my coat on the freestanding coat hook, and no one would have an inkling I was there. Then, I'd spread my books out and pore over my studies with a cigarette and a cup of coffee.

It was the springtime of my life and I counted the hours until I'd be back in Mandy's arms.

Then, in early April, disaster struck. I remember it all too well. I had just finished breakfast at Tehaan's when I got a *réveil pénible*, a rude awakening.

"Hey, MacKenzie," called Egley in a grating voice that made my hair stand on end. "So this is where you've been holed up."

My heart sank when I saw the thin-faced weasel.

"Oh, hi."

"You're up shit's creek without a paddle, my friend."

I didn't react when Egley sat down across from me. It was galling having the little crud invade my space. Everything about him aroused aversion—especially the gloating intonation he put on "my friend."

"What are you talking about?"

"I'm talking about what I just heard from Fletch."

"Peter? What did he tell you?"

Egley turned his head. In profile, his eyes were opaque and snakelike.

"Spit it out, man. What did he tell you?"

Sted drummed his fingers on Teehan's Formica counter, and held an evil smirk.

"It looks like your career at Georgetown is about to end."

"What makes you say that?"

"Gobbler Gribbet freaked out on the acid you gave him. Try 'sale of illegal drugs' on for size."

I crumpled at this piece of news. I felt like I'd been tagged with a body shot.

"I never gave Gobbler dick."

"Well, Fletch did."

"That was months ago."

Sted smiled luridly. He had the tendresse of a paparazzo. I wanted to smash his rodent face in.

"Gobbler was at Bevin Bledsoe's when he dropped."

"*Who the fuck* is Bevin Bledsoe?"

"Oh, he's only the Yard muckety-muck, you dimwad."

I stared in bewilderment. "He's a groundskeeper?"

Egley laughed.

"He's the Yard President."

I felt a blow in the pit of my stomach. "Yard President" was *hoyaspeak* for president of the student council.

"Oh, fuck."

"It gets worse. Gobbler drops the acid, goes 'PEEP PEEP PEEP PEEP' for six hours, and then wets his pants."

"You're lying, Egley."

"I'm not. I swear to Christ. And I'm Catholic."

"So Bledsoe ratted us out?" I asked.

"*Gobbler*. He went to the school nurse and gave you both up."

"I gotta find Peter."

"Try Copley lawn. He's waxing his Sprite."

I paid the check and made a beeline for my mailbox in the dorm basement. Inside was a letter from the disciplinary board, ordering your humble servant to appear before them on the charge of: "SALE OF ILLEGAL DRUGS."

Ouch! That got my attention. Nothing drives home the fact that you're fucked like seeing it in print on official university stationery.

I could feel my breakfast congealing into an awful lump. That pseudo hipster, Gobbler. Giving acid to a Republican was like stoking a wolverine with locoweed.

Peter wasn't on Copley lawn. He was in the Quad with his car next to Dahlgren Chapel. I heard music as I walked up with a downcast look.

"PETER!"

He couldn't hear me. Edith Piaf was singing "Exodus" from the speakers he'd propped in our dorm window. *"Ils sont là-bas dans un soleil d'hiver,"* sang the Little Sparrow, who wasn't averse to giving herself shots of morphine right through her skirt.

"HEY, PETER!"

Peter had a chamois cloth going and was oblivious to the world. The Bugeye was a jewel when Peter kept her spiffed. British sports cars don't cut it with the high-rev tuner crowd. Nothing about the temperamental buggers endears them to gearheads brought up on Hondas and Miatas.

Ah, but you should've seen the Green Weenie. The car was green. So were the seats, dash, and even the munchkin engine block, with its dauntless SU carbs.

"'Klumphy only busts boozers at polo matches,'" I yelled.

Peter Fletcher stopped the chamois cloth in mid-stroke.

"'KLUMPHY ONLY BUSTS BOOZERS AT POLO MATCHES'—YOUR EXACT WORDS," I said.

Peter looked mildly annoyed. The muscles stood out on his tanned arms and legs as he continued polishing the bonnet of his pygmy roadster.

"What do you think?"

He stepped back, puffing for breath as we admired the sheen of

British racing green. The Brits only built the 1477-pound marvel from 1958 to 1961.

"She's a beauty."

"She is. Keeping her Bristol fashion takes a lot of elbow grease."

"Christ Jesus, Don Pedro. I think it's time we fall on our swords."

"We still have an ace up our sleeve," Peter winked.

"What might that be?" I asked.

"Sted Egley is going to bat for us. His old man went to Georgetown Prep with Klumphy. They're practically peas in a pod."

"Oh, man."

"Don't worry. We have Sted on our team."

"Great. We're facing Koufax with a Whiffle bat."

Now I really felt sick. I wanted Sted pleading our case like I wanted to wake up conjoined with Charles Manson.

"Let's go for a spin. It'll settle our nerves."

I hopped in the Sprite and held on as Peter pulled the starter and gave it the stick.

"Let's drive down K Street and scope out the secretaries. It's so nice, they'll be sunning themselves like lizards."

"I don't know."

It was hard arguing with Peter. He had such an invincible aura—much of which derived from his good looks.

"Let's get some Coors. Beer helps me think."

"Coors is scarce. We'll sooner find a unicorn."

Peter and I went to Dixie Liquor and bought *Löwenbräu*, which, happily, was still German in 1968 and kicked ass. Then we drove down M Street, towards Pennsylvania Avenue.

"It's a crime to drink this without *wurst*."

"God, Peter. How can you even think of food?"

"Oh, a big fat *bratwurst* with onions, ketchup and mustard. Yum!"

"I feel ill. I wish I could barf."

"You'll feel better if we smoke a joint."

"Pot *is* therapeutic," I said.

"We're going the wrong way."

"How can you tell?"

"We're headed into the riot zone."

"Aw, shit."

Peter toked from a roach clip as we drove up 14th Street past Newton through what was left of the inner city. Martin Luther King had been assassinated on Thursday, April 3, 1968, in Memphis. Bloody riots exploded across America as blacks expressed their outrage.

"Jesus Christ, Dougie. It looks like Dresden."

"Imagine the rage it takes to burn down your own neighborhood."

When the riots started, cowardly whites fled town in droves, with yours truly leading the way.

"This is so ultra bogus, Doug."

"I know, man."

"Check it out. We spend the entire term *drunk*."

"Drunk off our asses."

"And they want to kick us out for pot."

"That's Jesuit logic."

"Are you hungry, yet?"

"I'm starved."

"Let's go to The Tombs and bag some burgs."

"I'd rather go to Clyde's and bag some babes."

"At a time of national mourning?"

"Sperm never sleeps."

"One thing we're *not* going to do is go see the dean."

Getting the Hose

It rubs the lotion on its skin, or else it gets the hose again.
—*Jame Gumb, The Silence of the Lambs*

"You can't wear your tenement tee shirt to see the dean."

Peter blew noisily in disgust.

"Why the hell not?"

"You look like you fell off the fire escape."

"Let's not make a big production out of this."

"You need a shower. You smell like Coppertone."

Peter gave his underarms cursory sniffs as I fumbled frantically with my tie.

"Your hands are shaking. Let me do that."

Peter tried to get my tie straight.

"Make it a double Windsor, would you?" I said.

"There. *Perfecto.*"

"Thanks. Now get it in gear."

"Relax. You worry too much. Dean Klumph likes people he can impress. And there aren't many of those around."

"Shake a leg, Pete."

"Here's the plan. We'll be fashionably late. Then, we'll breeze in and be deferential. It'll work."

"Right. We're fashionably late for the Nuremberg Trials? Then, we waltz in like 'The Blue Danube'?"

"Correct. Cutting a fine figure is the name of the game."

"I see. French cuffs win the day. What if Klumphy bangs his shoe, like Khrushchev?"

"He won't. Guess who he chummed around with at Canterbury?"

"Don't tell me. Sted Egley's old man."

Peter was dumbfounded. "How did you know?"

"You told me. Only last time you said they were chummy at Georgetown Prep. Remember?"

"Sted lied," croaked Peter. "His father doesn't know the Little Red Hen. Oh, shit. We're screwed. Klumph will ream our hinders. *After* my old man kills me."

Peter went deathly pale. He collapsed with an Olive Oyl groan.

"It's time to face the music," I said. "Let's boogie." Our loafers clicked on the marble floor as we marched down the hall towards the dean's office.

Our meeting did not go well. I sensed from Dean Klumph's icy glare that the topography of our mortal coils filled him with something less than delight.

"You do know what this is about?" said the dean.

Peter managed a brittle smile. He squirmed in Klumph's plush leather chair.

"Yes, sir," he said with a sappy rectitude. "I hope we haven't inconvenienced you in any way."

Klumph glared.

"I'm going to ask you some questions, and I want you to tell me the truth."

Peter and I exchanged nervous glances. We nodded compliantly.

"How many pushers do we have on campus?"

We could barely score enough weed to stay stoned, but Klumphy had us down for Frog One and Pablo Escobar.

"I don't know," shrugged Peter. "Honestly, I don't."

"Me, neither," I added truthfully.

Klumph scowled. He had a yellow pencil and made a big deal out of scribbling something.

"Give me a concrete figure," he said with a toplofty air.

I made the mistake of scrutinizing Klumph's sports jacket. It looked like it was made of worsted burlap. I've seen classier tailoring on goat blankets.

"Give me a number," barked the dean. "How many pushers?"

Klumphy was playing J. Edgar Hoover.

"You're not leaving this office until you give me a number."

Regis Klumph, Dean of Men, was right up there with Elmer Fudd, Dean of Rabbits.

"We'll stay here all day if we have to."

Peter and I sat staring numbly for what seemed an eternity.

"How many? Five to ten? Ten to fifteen? Fifteen to twenty? Twenty to twenty-five? Twenty-five to thirty?"

"Thirty-five to forty," upped Peter, deadpan.

Klumphy's eyes widened. Peter shot me a sly wink.

"Thirty-five to forty?" repeated Klumph elatedly.

We nearly bit through our lips as Dean Klumph scrunched down and scribbled away. From the look on his face you'd've thought he'd single-handedly cracked the Enigma code.

"Are they marijuana pushers or LSD pushers?"

"That depends," said Peter.

"Depends on what?"

"Well, obviously it depends on how they're dressed."

"I see. What would a marijuana pusher wear?"

I listened in disbelief as Peter fed Klumphy what sounded like a description of Dizzy Gillespie.

"And how would he differ from an LSD pusher?"

"An LSD pusher is impossible to detect," said Peter.

Klumphy stiffened. "Why is that?"

"Because he blends in like 'John Q. Citizen.'"

"Or a KGB mole," piped Klumphy.

"Precisely. Hence the term 'travel agent.'"

"LSD pushers are called 'travel agents'?"

"*Travel agents*?" Hoo, boy. Peter was quoting a record we used to play for laughs—an LP called "LSD"—and a blatant attempt to cash in on the "LSD craze" that was "sweeping college campuses." LSD users, it claimed, "howled" and "ate tree bark." The drug was sold by "travel agents"—shadowy characters with berets and bongo drums. A picture on the album cover showed an actual LSD user lying on the floor in an unidentified liquid.

LSD was noteworthy as the first outlawed substance that couldn't be blamed on the Negroes. The FBI couldn't find one Swiss chemist who was black.

"Are you prepared to name names?" Klumph asked.

Peter made a terrible face.

"Would you say MacKenzie is an LSD pusher?"

Peter's burst of candor surprised me. What he said next left me stunned.

"Douglas only sold pot. The LSD was all my doing."

Klumph leaned back, licking his chops.

"I only had ten tabs of acid," Peter whined pitifully.

"I'll let you discuss that with the Disciplinary Board."

I felt my throat close. Peter's jaw dropped.

"Isn't that rather... drastic?" pleaded Peter.

I winced at the thought of facing those Robespierre fleabags.

"My work here is over," said the dean.

Peter started screeching. He sounded like Peking opera.

"I did not sell Clark the LSD," he sobbed.

"Well, he didn't get it from The Campus Corner," said the dean.

"He *asked* me for it, and I gave it to him."

"You made your bed, son. You lie in it."

"But, sir, LSD was legal last year. Everybody tried it."

Klumph was unmoved.

"This will kill me. You don't understand. We have a legacy. My father went to school here, and his father before him."

Peter's pleadings were hopeless. There was a vermin rapacity about Klumph that was impervious to logic.

"If you scuttle my career at Georgetown, I'm ruined. Don't do this, Dean Klumph," he begged. "That's all I'm asking. Please give me another chance. I promise you, you won't be sorry."

Peter wept openly. Klumph brushed his sleeves with an impatient air. It was GAME OVER, but Peter wouldn't cop to it.

"I'm a Hoya, damn it, and I'll always be a Hoya. No one is more a Hoya than me. Not even Jack the Bulldog."

Klumph scribbled self-importantly on his legal pad.

"This meeting is adjourned."

Peter grew raspy as his poise guttered. Klumph was not going to warm to him on any level. Peter was a dope peddler with a Racquet Club accent. And Klumphy was a hireling stooge with a Jack Webb complex.

And it was 1968. Bloody 1968. The Tet Offensive signaled the Vietnam War was lost, yet the carnage continued until the fall of Saigon in 1975. Robert McNamara had LBJ's ear and proved the worst adviser since Lady Macbeth. Later, Richard Nixon would implement a war plan so brain dead it made Pat Boone's heavy metal album seem a sound idea.

Outside the Dean's office, I beckoned Peter over to a quiet corner, where we lit our cigarettes.

"Why'd you spill the beans like that?"

Peter shrugged. He smiled with wry detachment.

"He had us dead to rights. I thought it best to fess up."

"Well, thanks for telling me, you moron," I said.

"They're allowing us to resign."

"We could've done that on our own."

"Let's bolt. I could use some air."

Peter and I were in the soup. We walked outside Old North and watched some yellow bulldozers work on the site of the new Lauinger Library.

Looking down into the pit, he said, "Can you see any future in this muddy trench?"

I was at a loss for words. We both just stared into the pit. Peter was drawn and pale. I was numb.

"Klumph fucked us like inflatable sheep," said Peter finally. "Holy hell. What am I gonna' tell the old man?"

Peter's dad reminded me of Mr. Monopoly, that mustachioed little gent in the Monopoly game.

"Tell him the truth," I offered.

Ambassador Fletcher would be, rightly, aghast. He might have trouble finishing his lobster thermidor.

"I'm not going to Vietnam," I said. "I've got a better idea. We enroll at Bermuda Shorts Junior College. Take some easy courses. Keep up our grades. Cool our heels. Keep our noses clean. Let things die down."

"Wait for Curtis LeMay to nuke Hanoi."

"Then we re-apply," I exclaimed. "Clean cut. Madison Avenue. Bingo! We're in."

"And the chicks will be younger, so we'll really get some action."

Peter folded his arms and sighed. He looked skeptical.

"Forget it, Douglas. I could give a rat's ass about college. Georgetown can take a 'flying Rimbaud at the moon.'"

"What about your career in foreign service?" I asked.

"Do you really think I'd make a good diplomat? Everyone hates me."

"How can you say that? You're the caped crusader."

Peter looked away. His eyes were wildly sad. He clung to the wire fence as though he was imprisoned by it.

"Everybody gets crucified in boarding school, Peter. Even the great Stirling Moss. Stirling was deeply hurt when the other kids called him a 'Yid,' and a 'Jew-boy.'"

Peter sighed, betraying some terrible pain.

"That was awful about Clark," he said solemnly.

"Gobbler? He'll get over it."

"No. Jim Clark. Didn't you hear?"

The Lauinger Library bulldozer noise was drowning him out.

"DIDN'T I HEAR WHAT?"

"JIM CLARK DIED IN A FORMULA TWO RACE."

"WHAT?"

The bulldozer stopped before Peter could lower his voice.

"JIM CLARK WAS KILLED YESTERDAY."

"Where?"

"Hockenheim. It's a new racecourse in Germany."

"I don't believe it."

I looked pleadingly at Peter. His sad face hit home.

"A rear tire went flat. Clark went into the trees on the fastest part of the circuit."

I was staggered. Jim Clark was my hero. He made everyone proud to be Scottish. Scotland is a wee country, but it's given the world some amazing people.

"We still have Jackie Stewart. Thank God for that."

"Let's go to The Tombs. I'll buy you a beer."

Peter and I raised our glasses to Jim Clark. The little sheep farmer from Duns would always live in our hearts.

"Cripes! What'll we tell the parents?" asked Peter.

"We could tell them the truth."

"They don't even know I smoke pot."

"Here comes the Prodigal Son routine."

My dad was having a sandwich at the kitchen table when I straggled home.

"I love you, Daddy," I said as I kissed his bald head.

No more words were spoken. I gave him a hug from behind.

"Did you hear about Jim Clark?" was all I said.

Dad nodded. He never mentioned school. He was too classy for that.

<hr />

I managed to get back into Georgetown in 1974, but I had to see the new dean first because Klumphy sabotaged my transcript.

"Dean Cloke?"

"Yes?"

"I'm Doug MacKenzie. I have an appointment to see you."

Dean Cloke was a pleasant fellow with a friendly manner and a warm handshake.

"Have a seat, Doug."

I sank into a cool leather chair and steadied myself with deep breaths as the dean studied my file.

"You have 'NEVER TO BE RE-ADMITTED' on your transcript."

"It's an old transcript," I said dismissively.

Dean Cloke held a half smile. He parsed my shoddy record. "It appears you never got a grade higher than a 'C'?"

"I guess not."

"So you were in academic trouble before the disciplinary problem?"

"Pretty much."

"That is not good."

"No, sir."

I wanted to blurt out that I'd made it to the Fifth Level of the Alliance Française before being admitted to the Sorbonne. But I held my tongue.

"Are you presently employed?"

"Yes, sir. I'm a licensed restaurant manager. I work at The Guards in Georgetown, and at The East India Club."

"I love The Guards. They have fabulous steaks."

"And an awesome salad bar," I added proudly.

"The East India Club? I don't know that one."

I breathed a sigh of relief. The East India Club was more familiarly known as "The East Idiot Club" after a street creep slashed our bartender's cheek with a straight razor.

"It's a disco, sir. Downstairs from The Guards."

Dean Cloke was an upright hombre. I couldn't picture him in a zebra banquette, shoveling blow up his sneezer.

"What did you do before you were a restaurant manager?"

"I was in real estate."

"In what capacity?"

"Sales."

"How'd you like it?"

"Residential real estate is a challenge."

"The old smile and a shoeshine?"

"I knocked on a lot of doors."

"I'll bet you knocked 'em dead."

"I did my best."

My real estate career was a resounding dud. I couldn't have sold picnic lunches to the Donner Party.

"Think you might give it another whirl?"

Dean Cloke gave me a chummy wink. He looked ready to chuck me on the arm.

"Maybe."

I despised real estate. I loathed business. And I hated wearing a suit.

"So, Doug. What do you see as a career?"

"I want to be a novelist, sir."

Dean Cloke rubbed his chin. His dubious gaze made me regret I hadn't come up with a more pragmatic career choice. Saying I wanted to write novels sounded dippy. Like I wanted to make scented candles or balloon animals.

"Then, do it, Doug. Write your novel."

I nodded, smiling. But I wasn't quite sure what he meant. I thought he was blowing me off.

Then, he extended his hand, and he said with a big grin, "The Sixties are over. Welcome back."

"Thanks," I said, shaking his hand.

I walked outside and joyfully bounded across the lawn like my legs were on springs. It was *Miller* Time.

——•——

Georgetown came through for me in 1974, the summer Daddy died. If it didn't plop me on the literary path, it piped me to the pastures where the path could be found.

My dream of becoming a great fiction writer didn't pan out. Oscar Wilde said that there are two kinds of novelists: the unread and the unreadable. I managed to become both. But I can't complain. I chose a life of letters, and in the words of Merle Haggard, "I Take a Lot of Pride in What I Am."

Life was good to me. Thanks in great part to a supportive mother, I was able to follow my nature. Denying your dreams is the worst mistake you can make. If you're an artist, be an artist.

So, in the words of the immortal bard, "This above all, to thine own self be true." Take this wisdom to heart, and it will make all the difference.

IN TRIBUTE

In memory of my dear mother, Millicent deButts MacKenzie West.

"I am the utter poverty of God.
I am His emptiness, littleness, nothingness, lostness
When this is understood, my life in His freedom, the self emptying
of God in me is the fullness of Grace."
—Thomas Merton

and to "Scraps"

ACKNOWLEDGEMENTS

*To my editor Rachel Cartwright who helped guide "Mango Lassie"
every step of the way.*

To Mary Speer, a friend and colleague, and her dog, Clemenza.

To Nancy Lee and Howard Allen. Thanks for putting the "Fun" in Middleburg!

To Richard Holmes, family friend, and gardener for more than fifty years.

*To my dear friends Cynthia and Bob Quick in Santa Fe.
Thanks for so many laughs together.*

To my Sifu, Bi-Lian Lin, for the Tai Chi lessons and the watermelon.

*And to Kerry Manierre, who helped me find my way back
into the light when my mother died.*

ABOUT THE AUTHOR

Dougie MacKenzie was born in Washington, D.C. He grew up in Middleburg, Virginia and was educated at Georgetown University and the Sorbonne.

A celebrated playwright, he was *Pasatiempo* Magazine's 1988 Santa Fe Signature Artist for Writing. His work includes: *The Water Gators in Hell* (1977), an epic poem, and two plays, "The Splendid Wren," which opened at The Santa Fe Playhouse in 1996, and the acclaimed "Baby Rugby," which had its debut at The Armory for the Arts Theatre in Santa Fe, in 1998. The play received plaudits from theatre critic Craig Smith in *The New Mexican*.

MacKenzie began writing his memoir, *Mango Lassie,* while still a resident of Santa Fe.

"What I miss most about Santa Fe are the sunsets, the green chile and the good vibes," he says. "Santa Fe is the elephant graveyard for Sixties freaks. Flower Power is thriving in New Mexico. So is the art world. If you can't find inspiration in the Land Of Enchantment, you'd better hang it up."

"I lived the writer's life also in Paris, Rome, and London, and they can't touch Santa Fe. I owe my inspiration to twenty-three years of Santa Fe mornings."

Dougie MacKenzie lives in Purcellville, Virginia with his loquacious Burmese cat, Simon.

*My great grandfather, Hugh MacKenzie, emigrated to America from
Aberdeen, Scotland at age twelve.
He opened a fine leather goods store in Cincinnati, Ohio.*

The Tolman Laundry, founded in 1874
by James Perkins Tolman on Capitol Hill, Washington, D.C.

Edward Mills Tolman
My grandmother Edith Tolman's father (1879)

Edith Helen Tolman, my paternal grandmother at age four,
with her grandfather, James Perkins Tolman (September 23, 1881)

The Berlin-born tragedian, Richard Mansfield (1854–1907),
was my grandmother, Edith Tolman's first cousin. The New York Times said that,
"as an interpreter of Shakespeare, Mansfield had no living equal.
He was the greatest actor of his hour, and one of the greatest of all times."

The family, at Ingomar Street, N.W., Washington., D.C.
(l-r) my uncle, Albert "Burr" MacKenzie, my grandmother, Edith "Ba" MacKenzie,
my father, Don MacKenzie, my grandfather, Frederick MacKenzie,
and my aunt Caroline "Pie" MacKenzie

My father, Donald Frederick MacKenzie, above, as a student at Central High School, Washington, D.C. (1921). Young Don MacKenzie was president of his radio club, and a running back for the Chevy Chase Midgets.

Millicent Welby deButts, R.N. My wonderful mother, shown here, at left, in 1944, at age 23. A graduate (1941) of Garfield Hospital Nursing School, Washington, D.C.

Hunt Meet
Millicent MacKenzie with our friend and neighbor, Freddie Warburg (1949)

*Dad, Don MacKenzie, (left) at "Journey's End," Middleburg, Virginia,
with Daniel Cox Sands, MFH, the Middleburg Hunt. Mr. Sands, horse racing and
fox hunting luminary, also known as Mr. Middleburg, donated
Glenwood Park race course to the area. (January, 1949)*

Our family home, "Journey's End," Middleburg, Virginia

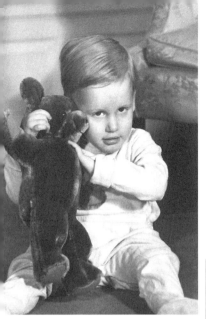

Doug MacKenzie, left, at age 2 (1950)

Mom and Dad, below, at The Middleburg
Hunt Ball (1949)

"Where'd They Go?"
My stepfather, Master of "Dinwiddie," William H. West, Jr.
cubbing with The Middleburg Hunt (1950)

My sister, Gail MacKenzie,
marries Marine Lieutenant Chris Slonaker (1952)

The MacKenzie Clan, inset (l-r), Ross, Doug, Niki and Bruce
"Journey's End" (1953)

Foxcroft Pony Club, above, Millicent MacKenzie with sons, Doug on "Little Better,"
and Ross on "Penny MacKenzie" (1953)

The Hill School Debate Team, inset, Doug MacKenzie, debate captain for Nixon, squares off with Jeanne Moon, captain for Kennedy (1960)

President John F. Kennedy, above, leaving Mass at the Middleburg Community Center (February, 1963) (photo by Howard Allen)

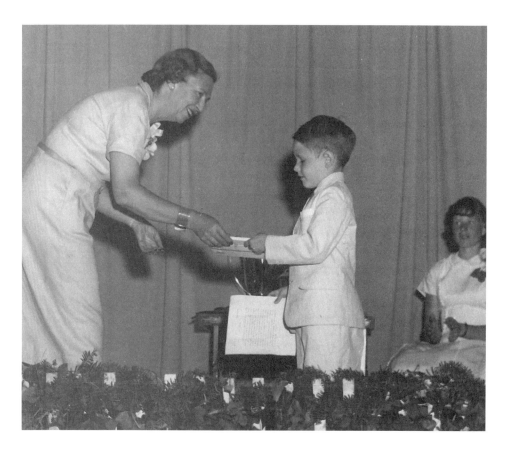

Doug MacKenzie wins the Prize Composition in the first grade,
accepting the award from Miss Anne Gochnauer,
Hill School, Middleburg, Virginia (1954)

Doug MacKenzie, top, first-year rat at RMA (1962)

My dog, "Shep," inset, at "Journey's End" (1964)

Don MacKenzie, President of the Middleburg National Bank, above, shown here at work.
Dad gave his opinion of the town in Sports Illustrated magazine (February 11, 1963)
"Take away the horse and do you know what's left? Nothing."

Episcopal High Senior, Bruce MacKenzie, cuts a rug with a Virginia belle
Middleburg Community Center (1959)

Three Middleburg foxes: Mom and friends
(l-r) Alice Mills, Millicent MacKenzie, and Rosalie Grasty

Mom's friend, Pamela Harriman, bought "Journey's End" in 1977

AIFS kids, top, sharing a laugh at Sacré-Coeur, Paris (August 1966)

Student ID card, above, Paris (1971-1972)

*My Mango Lassie, right, Mandy Pringle
after a Georgetown party, Washington, D.C.*

Mandy Pringle, below, as she lived and loved

"Weasels ripped my shorts"
Doug MacKenzie and the "Plastic Pig," his '66 Vette (1978)

Doug MacKenzie and "Babs," a California bunny,
in Santa Fe (1993)

Mom, with First Lady Hillary Rodham Clinton
The White House, American Academy in Rome 100th Anniversary (April 21, 1994)